ON THE TRACK OF PREHISTORIC MAN

by HERBERT KÜHN

"My aim," says the author, "is to tell of the times when man emerged from the darkness—before he was caught in the light of history."

This unique book tells the fascinating story of those murky, twilit days when man was first groping his way toward the beginnings of civilization. It is the story of the birth and flowering of man's first great art achievements, many tens of thousands of years ago.

It is also the story of those unknown hunters, wizards, artists, medicine men and ordinary folk who lived and worshipped in the vast caverns of the Ice Age. Beset by huge bears and lions and woolly mammoths, dependent for food upon giant stags, wild bulls and horses, these early humans yet managed to leave some astonishing examples of art, many of which have been unsurpassed for twenty thousand years.

ON
THE
TRACK
OF
PREHISTORIC
MAN

Herbert Kühn

Translated from the German by
Alan Houghton Brodrick

PUBLISHED BY RANDOM HOUSE
New York

Random House IS THE PUBLISHER OF *The Modern Library*

BENNETT CERF • DONALD S. KLOPFER

Manufactured in the United States of America by H. Wolff

Contents

DRAWINGS

MAPS AND GROUND PLANS

The subject of this book is a region where life on this earth reveals one of its greatest mysteries; that is to say, where mankind became fully human. My aim is to tell of the times when Man emerged from the darkness—but before he was caught in the light of history: of the epochs that lie before tradition.

Beasts live in the present, they know only the here and the now, but Man—and that constitutes his peculiar quality—thinks of the future, thinks also of the past. And not only of days, weeks and years, but of the ever recurring, of the ever present, problem of birth and death.

We cannot conceive of our own beginning or of our own death. Though we may see men die and see men born, that does not make our own beginning or our own end any more real.

Yet there is not one of us who does not wish to know how this race arose that now peoples the globe. In former days, when these thoughts assailed us, we read in ancient books, in the Bible, in ancient Egyptian papyri, in the clay tablets of the Sumerians, in the early records of the Chinese. For ages some men believed these writings while others were pleased to feel such things were only fables.

And while the ultimate mystery will be forever veiled for us, we can now see clear where only a generation or two ago all seemed obscure. Just as the microscope has enlightened us about the mysteries of the birth of the individual, so now we can view what none before us have seen.

Wherever men have lived upon this earth they have left traces of their presence, and these traces have been preserved: bones, skulls, teeth, stone instruments, articles of adornment, dwellings, settlements. We can lift up the earth in layers and spread it out so that we can read it as a book in which is chronicled what men did who lived millennia before us, our forefathers from whom we are derived.

Of course, all the problems of archaeology are far from

having been solved; new ones are always appearing; still, very much has already been learnt. The archaeologist stands before this "book" just as the man at the microscope gazes at a universe in a drop of water. This present volume, it is hoped, will reveal something of what has been discovered concerning the life of prehistoric men, of their creations and of their hopes and fears.

H. K.

I: Lascaux

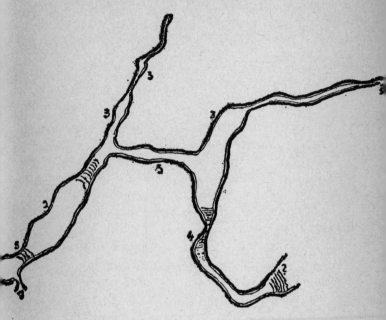

Ground plan of the Lascaux Cave, near Montignac, Dordogne Department, France: (1) Entrance. (2) Main hall with paintings. (3) Paintings. (4) Bison and Man. (5) Sorcerer.

A mild breeze was wafted through the open window of the Paris-Toulouse train compartment as I sat watching the pleasing landscape, the delightful woods, the fresh greenery, and that bright, diaphanous atmosphere which generations of painters have found so entrancing. Everything looked delicate and tender. No gloomy fir-forests, no deep, sad shadows at eventide. A landscape of poplars and meadows, of graceful trees whose fragile, quivering branches bore soft veils of shade. I thought to myself, "This is the effect

Corot painted; here are the Impressionists' lights and colors; those trees, there, belong to Courbet, to Renoir, to Manet."

And all the time I was filled with expectation and excitement. My goal was a newly discovered cavern decorated with great pictures, polychrome paintings of Ice Age date: the cave of Lascaux, near Montignac, which, because of the war, I had not been able to visit before this, though it was found in 1940.

Ever since I had first heard of Lascaux I had been most anxious to see these new marvels in the bowels of the earth. All my life I had studied the last Ice Age and written about it—had published a number of books about it, in fact. I had visited all the prehistoric painted or engraved caves that were known before the 1939-45 war. In many, if not in most, of these caverns I had, in company with Frenchmen or Spaniards, conducted excavations. Ever present in my mind had been the problems connected with late palaeolithic or Ice Age Man, problems relating to the inhabitants of Europe at a time when the northern and central parts of the continent were covered with ice and glaciers; men who lived with the great beasts in the rigorous climate of later Old Stone Age times, beasts which, most of them, have long since been extinct in our lands: mammoths, reindeer, rhinoceroses, bisons, snowy owls, and giant stags. The Europe of those days showed a face very different from that in our times. Not only, of course, were there no towns or villages, but men did not know the use of metals and had not yet begun to fashion vessels of pottery, those utensils whose shards and fragments, belonging to later epochs, are so often found in the earth. Man was forced to accept what nature offered him. He subsisted on plants and roots, on snails—and on the wild animals in whose midst he lived.

Of course the most important foodstuffs were furnished by animals. Therefore men's thoughts were centered upon the chase. If a man could not kill game he himself could not live. Moreover, not only did the animals serve as food but their skins and furs were used as clothing. With bones and horns and antlers men made instruments and tools. Animal fat fed the oil lamps needed for lighting the caves, since much of men's lives was spent in caverns which served as asylums and dwellings, as houses and huts. It is true that the foundations of shelters have been found near summer hunting-grounds, up near the ice-line. Such shelters were composed of pits or trenches dug down into the earth and completed above with twigs and branches supported on stakes driven into the ground. With the tools man had at his disposal in those days, however, the building of such pit-dwellings must have been a lengthy and tedious job. So when caves were available men seized the opportunity of occupying such comfortable and, generally speaking, desirable quarters. And it is because of man's cave-dwelling habits that the traces of our ancestors have been preserved. In the caves fillings were formed, fillings made up of layers or strata containing discarded instruments, tools, and other objects utilized in everyday life. Dust, sand, and earth blown or washed in through the caves' mouths laid down and preserved for us a clearly marked succession of strata which we can read as we can a book, each leaf being a layer with proof and evidence of men's lives and works. One cannot help thinking what a very lucky thing it was that in the Middle Ages men did not trouble much about visiting caves, and bothered still less about digging in them.

But for a hundred years now archaeologists have been digging in caves, and so, after a century, it is possible to get a good general idea of the results obtained.

Four times during the Pleistocene, or latest geological period (except of course the Holocene, or Recent, in which we are living), Ice Ages swept across Europe. The first (or Günz) may have begun about 600,000 years ago.* The

* The figures given for the Ice Ages are those arrived at by calculations (based on differences in the intensity of the sun's radiation) generally associated with the name of Milankovich. The figures are, of course, only tentative and have not found acceptance by all prehistorians and archaeologists. (*Translator's note.*)

second (or Mindel) Ice Age may have started some 400,000 years ago, the third (or Riss Glaciation) approximately 200,000 years ago, and the fourth, and last (or Würm Glaciation), began possibly about 100,000 years ago. It is this last Glaciation which is commonly referred to as the "Ice Age," and throughout this book the words "Ice Age," when used alone, relate only to this last, Würm, Glaciation. During the earlier part of the last Ice Age, a type of man known as the Neanderthaloid flourished in Europe. These men are so called because the first of their skeletons to be recovered was that found at a cave in the Neanderthal, not far from Düsseldorf, in 1856. It is clear, however, that men of Neanderthaloid type lived in Europe before the beginning of the last Ice Age, just as it is evident that "modern" men—that is, men of a type comparable with the human beings now living on the earth—also flourished in Europe during the so-called Interglacial or warm period between the two last Ice Ages. However, "modern" man spread widely (and eventually absorbed, or displaced, the Neanderthaloids) during the middle and the latter part of the last Ice Age. The most celebrated type of such "modern" men is the so-called Cro-Magnon, now known from over one hundred skeletons or portions of skeletons.

Men of this "modern" type (the name "Cro-Magnon," like "Neanderthaloids," is taken from the name of the site where the first discoveries of bones of this type of "modern" man were made) are of immense significance to us, because they were artists.

When, over a hundred years ago, the archaeologists during their excavations came across the first bones of mammoth, rhinoceros, and reindeer, associated with instruments quite obviously made by human agency, much discussion at once arose as to whether man had actually lived during the Ice Age, and at the same period as these extinct animals. No evidence seemed to settle the question one way or another.

It may be imagined, then, how great was the excitement

when in 1864 Lartet discovered in the La Madeleine cave a piece of mammoth-bone engraved with the figure of a mammoth.

The proof, so long awaited, was at last forthcoming. Without any shadow of a doubt prehistoric man had lived at the same time as the mammoth in western Europe. Lartet's delight at his solution of the puzzle was obvious from the wording of his report, in which he showed himself very pleased indeed that he had been able to overcome the obstinate prejudices of his day.

Since Lartet's time it has become abundantly clear that late palaeolithic men were artists who drew and painted the world they saw around them; for after a number of further excavations resulting in the discovery of more and more small art-objects in or on stone and bone, there came the great day in 1901 when caves were found adorned with splendid prehistoric paintings.

The first of these prehistoric picture-galleries was, of course, Altamira. It is true that it had been discovered in 1879, but later on it had been completely forgotten.

During the half-century from 1903 to 1953 there were recognized no less than one hundred and seven caverns in which Ice Age paintings and engravings could be seen. Many of the caves, indeed, contained hundreds of pictures. Through this abundance of material we are able today to gain such a clear and close impression of how Ice Age men lived that, in imagination, we can stand near them and, so to speak, look over their shoulders while they work. Naturally, not all the caves can rival the marvels of Altamira, which has been called the "Sistine Chapel" of prehistoric art. And it cannot be too often repeated that the impression left by the paintings of Altamira is overwhelming.

Such thoughts kept running through my mind as I sat in the train while it sped southward from Paris. What would Lascaux be like? Newspapers had carried articles on it, reviews and magazines in America, France, Great Britain, and Germany had published illustrations of the Lascaux pictures. The whole scientific world had been excited by the discovery. On all sides there had appeared notices on Ice Age art. And now . . . well, the next day I too should be looking at Lascaux . . . what would the pictures mean for me?

The train pulled up at Brive station. Brive is a charming little town in west-central France and on the main Paris-Toulouse railway line. During the evening I walked about the streets and gazed in the attractive shop windows which, happily, once again displayed for sale every sort of produce and article the heart could desire.

The next morning I took the local train as far as Condat, where I caught the motor-bus for Montignac in the Dordogne department.

Montignac is an attractive place of about three thousand inhabitants. The motor-bus pulled up in front of an excellent hotel where I was shown into a good room. Then I asked how to get out to the cave. The landlord told me all about the excitement in the town when Lascaux was discovered, on September 12, 1940. Practically all the inhabitants of Montignac went out to see the buried pictures. Then he recounted how Breuil, the celebrated archaeologist, had arrived to visit the cave. In the presence of hundreds of visitors he had again and again explained the pictures and revealed their mysteries; he had spoken of the age of the paintings and of their meaning. Then my host gave me precise indications as to how to get out to the cave. As I walked along I could see photographs of Lascaux in almost every shop window.

It is impossible to lose one's way. All along the road signposts point toward the cave. One has the impression of being on the path to a pilgrimage shrine. In recent years a good motor road has been built out to Lascaux and during my short walk of not much more than twenty minutes I encountered a continuous stream of cars and buses headed for the grotto.

As you climb the hill you can see Montignac below you,

roofs and church tower, all set amid fields and undulating,
even hilly country such as one so often finds in central
France . . . soon, you get among the woods; first of all
deciduous trees and then, higher up, firs. At the end of
the path and on the down's ridge is an inn set among the
firs. There also is a parking space for cars . . . and the
entrance of the Cave of Lascaux.

You hardly notice this entrance until you come almost
right upon it, but when you are fairly close to it you can
see the new flight of steps built by the administration of
the *Monuments Historiques*, the Historical Monuments
Commission. You walk down the steps and are faced by
an iron door flanked by large and massive masonry blocks.
Through the door lies an antechamber, a large, dim hall in
which you can make out nothing until your eyes become
accustomed to the gloom. Then you are confronted with
yet another door which is never opened until the first is
carefully shut. As little fresh air as possible must be allowed
in, for variations in temperature would affect the paintings
most adversely.

The guides are four lads, four out of those who in 1940,
and quite by accident, stumbled upon the cave. I waited
until the main stream of visitors had passed in and on. Then
I introduced myself to the guides, told them I had come
from Germany, that I was professor of prehistory at the
University of Mainz and that I was very happy to find
myself just where, after long millennia, they had so to
speak seen the pictures rise out of the earth.

The young men were communicative enough and told
me the story of their adventures on that September day in
1940. They were playing about in the woods when their
dog, Robot, disappeared. They hunted about for him, and
then concluded that he had fallen down a hole no one up
to then had noticed. They set to work to tug out the scrub
blocking the hole and then threw a stone down it. The
stone was a little time before it struck some hard object.
Ravidat, who was the eldest, if not the leader of the

group, gave me the most details. "I took a big knife, cut away the weeds, and moved stones until the hole was big enough for me to slither in; but, at the beginning, I had to ease myself in rather sideways. I contracted my shoulders and wriggled like a snake forward on my belly for perhaps six or seven yards. Then I pulled out my pocket flashlight but, at that moment, a stone gave way. I lost my balance and slipped down into the depths—perhaps forty or fifty feet. I was pretty well shaken when I got to the bottom but was glad to find that my flashlight was still in working order. By its light I could see I was in a cave. So I called up to the other boys, telling them to follow me down carefully and slowly. One after another they came along. Stones and gravel rattled and poured down with them, but soon enough we were all standing in a spacious hall, though we were bruised and bewildered.

"The walls, by our lamps' light, shone and shimmered. At first we didn't notice anything special, then suddenly we began to see lines on the rock walls. 'Look here,' said one of us, 'look over here, there are lots of lines here'—I turned my lamp toward the spot he indicated and there were, looming up, great enormous paintings of animals. One of us said, 'What about these being some of those prehistoric paintings?' . . . and we walked about the cave again and again while we shouted out in excitement as we found new pictures, more and more paintings of animals. We didn't try to hide our delight but patted each other on the back and danced a sort of Indian war-dance. There and then we took a solemn promise to each other that we would not breathe to anyone a word of our discovery but that we'd come back the next day with lamps. And the very next morning we began the systematic exploration of the whole cavern. You can imagine how our fever of excitement rose as we beheld ever more and more pictures!

"Presently we came to a place where the ground suddenly dropped away steeply downward. As I was the strongest I decided that I should be the first to dive down into the dark depths. My heart beat fast enough, you can be sure, for you never know what you're going to come up against in caves and very often they've got uncanny and unexpected things that may be impressive and exciting enough, but also pretty dangerous. I slithered down, grabbing as best I could onto the irregularities of the rock-face and, after all, came safely down below onto firm ground, where I saw an extraordinary picture: a human form with a bird's head lying on its back and menaced, attacked by a bison."

Ravidat broke off his tale, but it was clear how excited he was by the mere memory of the heroic days in 1940.

My own excitement gained on me. I had of course seen plenty of photographs of the cave. I had published in *IPEK* (*Annual of Prehistoric and Ethnographic Art*) an article on Lascaux by Martínez Santa-Olalla of Madrid. Now, however, I myself was about to see the originals, to stand before the mysterious marvels. When the second door opened I stopped still, arrested, as I suppose most visitors are, by the overwhelming vision.

A large chamber, long and oval. The upper part of the walls and the vaulting of the roof covered with pictures. A veritable painted sanctuary. From the whole assemblage emanates a sense of the sacred, and to my mind, perhaps oddly enough, the electric lighting which has been installed rather increases than diminishes this impression of the hallowed character of the place. The lamps are hidden in the ground and the light they cast upon the pictures is soft, though they stand out sharp and plainly visible. There is nothing garish; the atmosphere of dim antiquity, of remoteness from this world of ours—all that is unaltered.

Quite near the entrance is a portrait of a wizard, most probably painted by himself. He wears a beast's skin and the mask of some fantastic animal which never yet existed, a creature with long, thick horns . . . and all about are the huge aurochs, stags, wild horses. You cannot imagine beforehand what your eye will light upon next. Many of the paintings are executed in rather blurred technique, so softly, so lightly that these animals with black heads and yellow bodies remind you of Japanese India-ink paintings. Most of the figures have lengths of between three and six feet, though some of the pictures are fifteen and even twenty feet long and the great frieze depicting heads of swimming stags, for instance, measures more than fifteen feet. All these things are painted as though by a modern Impressionist. Nothing about them is "primitive," uncertain, unskillful. Everything is portrayed by artists who possessed full mastery over their materials and who had a close knowledge both of animal forms and of the laws governing representational art. The beasts are shown in repose, in space . . . the offside legs are clearly depicted and stand out in perspective while the hooves are painted so as to convey a most lifelike impression.

Some of the animals are looking about them, lifting their forelegs, running or galloping. Others again are in slow, striding movement, while yet others seem aware of possible danger and even look as though they are about to take cover. Among some of the most attractive of the Lascaux paintings are those of small wild horses, executed in an almost modern style.

There are also masses and masses of engravings, many of which are so inextricably intertwined with others that they are most difficult to identify. Ravidat—who, after all, has had plenty of opportunity to observe—is of the opinion that there are more than two thousand engravings on the cavern's walls. In many places the drawings lie over and under each other in a veritable maze. There is a good deal of overpainting, but that, in the case of the pictures, allows of some determination of the succeeding art-style periods. Such relative dating does not, of course, resolve the problem of the absolute dating of the Lascaux pictures.

Breuil—with whom I was able, later on, to engage in an exhaustive discussion regarding Lascaux—is of the opinion that the major portion of the paintings and engravings should be assigned to a middle period of the last Ice Age, that is to say, generally speaking, to the Aurignacian culture-complexes. This might make the oldest of the Lascaux works of art date from as much as 50,000 years ago. Against this view I would advance the opinion—and I think there are valid grounds to justify it—that the largest Lascaux pictures belong to the later phases of the upper palaeolithic or of the Ice Age. Moreover, I would set the age of such pictures at from about 15,000 to 10,000 B.C.; that is, they may well be from 17,000 to 12,000 years of age. It is true that under these large cartoons lie mid-Magdalenian paintings and below these again are some Aurignacian pictures. Of course, the whole problem calls for long and careful research. In any case, the Lascaux art-gallery contains specimens of the most magnificent art left to us by men of the Old Stone Age.*

What must strike every visitor to Lascaux is the quite astoundingly good state of the pictures' preservation. If, for instance, we look at Romanesque frescoes—paintings dating from about A.D. 1000 and even later—we are at once aware of the deterioration in their condition, a deterioration which, as we see it, is quite inevitable after the passage of ten centuries. Now, the Lascaux pictures, it is agreed,

* At this point in the text, the author adds the following sentence: "*In neuester Zeit ist eine genaue Untersuchung des Alters gemacht worden nach dem neuen Radiumkarbonverfahren*"; that is to say, "Quite recently a close enquiry" (or "an accurate investigation") "into the age has been made by the new radio-carbon process." As the full report on the Lascaux specimens was, perhaps, not received from Dr. Libby's laboratory at Chicago before the present book was written, it is only just to the author to add the following explanation. In 1951, the Abbé Breuil and M. Blanc excavated from the floor of the lower gallery, and in close proximity to the enigmatic fresco of the man and the bison, a number of stone "lamps" (i.e., concave slabs) together with some "assegais" of bone. With these finds were associated a good many lumps of charcoal. The radio-carbon (or carbon 14) test is a method of determining the age of any object of organic origin, and the test is proving of the greatest value in assessing the age of any such object whose life ceased not more than about 35,000 years ago. Charcoal is a particularly good material for radio-carbon tests, and the Lascaux charcoal gave a date of about 16,000 years. In other words, men were lighting fires at Lascaux 16,000 years ago—but we do not know, of course, if the charcoal was exactly contemporary with any of the pictures' execution. (*Translator's note.*)

may be anything up to 20,000 years old at least, and yet they are better preserved than almost any Romanesque painting we have. We are left gaping at the marvel for, indeed, the whole thing is rather mysterious.

The solution to the enigma must be sought in an appreciation of the physical conditions which prevailed in the cave, a cavern which lay hidden away in the earth, denied to men, hermetically sealed and so preserved from changes of temperature, of humidity, and of air. There is, as a matter of fact, a place at Lascaux where the pictures have been obliterated, and this is near a small opening or aperture through which cold winter air could seep in. It was even temperature that kept the pictures throughout the ages. No winter, no summer. Furthermore, the nature of the peculiarly hard Lascaux limestone is such that it permits of the formation of small, thin, transparent particles of calcite which much resemble tiny bits of glass. In this way, the paintings have become covered, in part at least, with a delicate coating that has maintained them as fresh as when they were limned. In fact the brilliance of the colors is almost incredible.

It is apparent that in many cases the artist, before he began painting, used a stone knife-blade to trace outlines upon the rock surface. It is clear, also, that these engraved lines were first of all marked out by means of a brush. We can be quite sure that a brush was used, for the lines are so thin that it would be impracticable, if not impossible, to make them with any other instrument than a brush. In German, one of a snipe's plumes is popularly called *die Malerfeder*, or "the artist's feather." Delicate feathers could be fixed into small bones and thus make very useful and handy brushes. Most of the pigments on the other hand appear to have been squirted onto the rock-surface, squirted in much the same way as we paint automobiles nowadays. The surface was prepared with fat and oil and then the powdered colors were blown onto the background thus made ready to receive them. It is most probable that blow-tubes of bone were utilized, since such objects have been recovered in great numbers from the filling-strata of other caverns. The Lascaux colors are thus real oil-colors comparable to those employed by artists at the present time; that is, pigments composed of ochres and animal fats. The ochres would have been pounded fine in mortars, and in many caves ochre-crayons have been found, ranging in tint from quite light to very dark. During excavations such pigments have turned up, neatly arranged in a row, just as a modern painter will arrange his tubes. Such objects have been discovered both at Mas d'Azil and at Altamira.

I must confess that, at first anyway, I wandered round the halls of Lascaux quite bemused. The millennia had rolled back and there were the men of the Ice Age, there, right near me. . . .

We used a rope-ladder to clamber down to the lower gallery where there is the picture of a man lying dead after having been attacked by a bison. A lance pierces the bison's flanks and the beast's bowels sag down from out of its belly. But the man lies stricken to death. Before him, on a pole, is a bird. We may puzzle a long time before we can read the riddle of this picture's significance. Is the bird the bird of the "soul"? Is it a representation of "death"? Anyway, whatever may be the precise significance of the painting we may be sure enough that the mysteries of existence, of birth and of death, were major marvels always looming above men of the late palaeolithic. Many, if not most, of these Lascaux beasts are pregnant and are obviously related to some fertility-magic. In many cases arrows are directed toward the animals and, then, we can see the snares into which they should fall . . . magic to encompass the destruction of game.

The Lascaux pictures, then, not only tell us a good deal about remote ages but also, what is more interesting to us, say something about the men themselves who lived here, thousands of years ago, in this lovely Vézère valley.

II: Les Eyzies

Meadows and wooded hills, country houses half-seen among the trees, red roofs and strange, box-shaped houses. Peasants in blue smocks perched upon high, two-wheeled carts.

Our train cut rapidly through the countryside. The sun sank blood-red behind the heights. Small wisps of cloud hung motionless over a horizon gilded by the last rays of sunset.

It was almost dark when we got to Bordeaux; we were off early the next morning for Périgueux, a fair-sized town in the department of the Dordogne, and the old capital of the province of Périgord. The Abbé Breuil had given us a word of introduction for M. Didon, the landlord of the Hôtel du Commerce, who was delighted to have news of his distinguished friend and who, himself, accompanied us to our rooms.

I can remember the date as though it were only yesterday: June 5, 1923.

"You're the first Germans to come to Périgueux since the war. If you want to visit the prehistoric sites, I can perhaps be of help to you. Indeed, I know them quite well. All those objects over there were found during my own excavations."

With these words he led us to some glass cases. On the shelves were flints, bone points and harpoons, all of late Old Stone Age, or Ice Age, date. "I also discovered a couple of art-objects, engravings of a very early period—Aurignacian, in fact. We found them in the Abri Blanchard but I gave them to the National Archaeological Museum at Saint-Germain."

While we were looking at the pieces, our landlord gave me a copy of his report on the excavation. I could not help thinking that we had come to the right place, without any doubt. Even the hotel-keepers here were amateur archaeologists interested in prehistory.

Early the next morning Didon ordered a car to take us to Les Eyzies. It was a marvelous day. The foliage fluttered in the fresh air. Dewdrops glittered and sparkled. Flowers twinkled among the grasses, while the river, the Vézère itself, lay like a silver ribbon flung upon the green fields. Soon the tall trees began to cast shadows upon the highway, and then the risen sun beamed clear and brilliant upon us. Before long the vale narrowed. Cliffs closed in upon the stream's course. We were entering the region that was a chosen realm of prehistoric Man, a paradise for our ancestors of late palaeolithic times. To our left were rock-faces looking southward, their overhanging ledges making natural shelters from wind and weather.

Then, quite suddenly, we noticed something very curious. Under the overhanging cliffs, and to the right and left, stretched lengths of primitive wall linked by an advanced fore-wall. And then there was the house. No roof was needed, no rear wall. On this very site and, indeed, in much the same sort of dwelling, lived the men of the last Ice Age. Our car pulled up. We were at La Laugerie Basse.

From the cottages rose columns of smoke that drifted along under the projecting ledge of rock, just as, no doubt, prehistoric men's smoke was wafted along ten thousand years ago. There were children playing, shouting and yelling as they tumbled out of the humble houses. . . . We began to make our way up the narrow path leading to the dwellings. On either side of the passageway lay stone instruments—artifacts—of Old Stone Age date. My pocket was full of them long before we reached the cottage. The door was open, and once we were inside we could see for ourselves that there was, indeed, no back wall. Its place was taken by the naked rocky cliff along which smoke from the big stove glided up and right out into the open air.

The floor, hardened by countless footsteps and quite innocent of covering, formed, moreover, a completely untouched prehistoric site dating from the last Ice Age. No one had ever excavated in the cottage, but a dig anywhere —say, right behind the front door— would have given remarkable results.

The owner, named Langlade, and his wife were sitting at the table. We passed the time of day. Then he led us to the rock-face, opened a door, and there we saw in the half-darkness a grotto extending far into the cliff. This was the famed prehistoric site of La Laugerie Basse. After fumbling about a bit with his lamp Langlade got it going and threw its beams right into the gaping cavity. We could see a fairly long way in. The strata, or levels, lie one above the other and are exposed like the leaves of a book. To indicate the different layers small signs have been set up, sticks bearing figures.

Salamander, Mid-Magdalenian, three-quarters actual size. La Laugerie Basse, Dordogne, France.

Meanwhile someone from the other side of the road was making his way up to the site. It was Peyrony, the local schoolmaster at Les Eyzies, and also the official overseer, or director, of excavations, who was in charge of all the prehistoric sites of the region. We walked toward him and told him who I was. When I put Breuil's letter into his hands, his eyes lit up. He greeted both of us warmly, as though we were old friends. Then, without more ado, he said, "The top layer here belongs to the late Magdalenian —which, as you know, was the last period of the Ice Age and is so named from the La Madeleine cliff-site that you'll be able to visit today. Such strata have, in a general way, yielded the finest works of art of any prehistoric epoch, and here at La Laugerie Basse this late Magdalenian stratum is almost inexhaustible. Digging has been going on ever since 1864, when Lartet first began his excavations here, and still something new is always turning up. A little later on you must examine something M. Maury—he's digging here now—unearthed not so long ago. It's a piece of reindeer horn carved into the figure of a salamander. It's a very beautiful object, and it comes from this very site."

He pointed toward the strata, at a spot which had obviously been worked recently.

"Would you like to help things forward a little? Here's a mattock, what we call a *crochet*."

Although we talk of "spadework," and "digging," the spade as a matter of fact is not much used in the excavation of prehistoric sites. A spade is too heavy and clumsy a tool to employ where small objects may be encountered. Instead, the excavator scratches with a miniature mattock. And he scratches very carefully indeed. Inch by inch the filling of a whole layer is loosened. Then the material thus prepared is smoothed out with a soft brush so that nothing can escape detection.

A minute or two after Peyrony had made his proposal, I was facing up to the stratum and warily scratching away with my mattock. In a trice there was a Magdalenian artifact in my hand. And this was my very first dig at an Ice Age site. There I was standing with my mattock in my hand and in the chosen field of prehistoric men—in fact, on classical ground for upper palaeolithic investigations. Before me, several generations of scientific investigators had stood in this very place and had been fired with the desire to find something which our far-off ancestors had held in their hands—a stone instrument, a splinter of bone, an art object. I must confess that my cheeks were burning with excitement and my hands were trembling a little. One of my dearest dreams had come true.

"And where was that stag found? You know the one I mean, the beast's got its head turned as though it were looking behind."

Peyrony pointed to a spot that had been cleared.

"And where did they discover that wonderful bison that was reproduced in 1916 in *L'Anthropologie* magazine?"

"Not far away from there. Borlon turned it up. That was a red-letter day for us. Quite near by was also a small stone engraved with the figure of a cave bear. You'll probably remember that the picture of this also appeared in the same article."

"Oh, yes, I remember quite well. I can see the figure now . . . how the stag is looking round . . . the wonderful skill with which the experience of a moment is conveyed. With a few strokes everything essential is presented. The whole thing is of the greatest aesthetic significance."

"Of course—like Nature itself. All those pieces were found in 1910. Those were the times. We lived through transports of joy—and then there was the head of a hind. We've got to admit that nowadays there aren't many artists who can draw like that. And only a little while ago M. Maury found several horses' heads and also a marvelously beautiful reindeer engraved on stone. They all turned up quite near where the 'lizard' was found."

And then, as we were talking, there was another stone artifact in my hand. A neatly worked scraper, the under face quite smooth, the upper face furnished with a ridge so as to allow the instrument to be grasped with the thumb and index finger. The whole thing had the form of a keel. Above, the flint was worked from top to bottom and marks of chipping were also visible on the sides.

"Monsieur Peyrony, look at what I've got here."

"Ah, yes, that's a *grattoir caréné*, a keel-shaped scraper. Many people seem to think that such scrapers are met with only in strata that lie deep down under the Magdalenian, but there you are—now, just look at this piece, another

Reindeer and trap, engraving on stone. Mid-Magdalenian, enlarged to about double actual size. La Laugerie Basse, Dordogne, France.

splendid scraper. Nevertheless, here at La Laugerie Basse there's nothing at all except Magdalenian. Of course it's always possible that down there, right down there beneath us, something else may some day come to light, but the layers that have been found, those which lie here right in front of us, belong, all of them, either to mid or late Magdalenian."

I cradled the stone instrument in my hand and looked at it. What could it have been used for? I fiddled about with it in all sorts of ways, but if held between thumb and forefinger, the tool was always the right way up. The under surface was smooth and shiny, so the artifact must have been used for scraping. I pushed the thing about back and forth on a large stone. Perhaps it was used to separate the pelt from the flesh. The instrument, indeed, was a sort of plane, possibly employed for smoothing out leather.

We worked at the site for a little longer. I dug up two more bone objects. A fine harpoon and then a long, sharp little needle with an eye. By this time M. Maury had arrived to take charge of us.

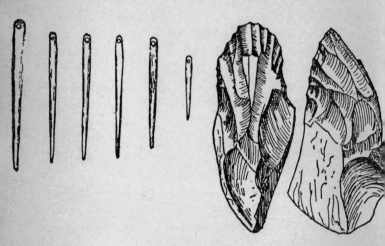

Left: *Sewing needles, half actual size. La Laugerie Basse, near Les Eyzies.* Right: *Scrapers, Aurignacian, from La Laugerie Basse, near Les Eyzies, Dordogne, France. Actual size.*

"Madame, the Ice Mother, used to sit here and sew for her baby. A nice tiny little fur coat. 'Oho, see how smart and pretty my baby looks in his new clothes,' she must have said. Monsieur, the Ice Daddy, drew himself up proudly as he stood beside them, and then he wiped the baby's little nose, for the weather was cold and the little nose was running," laughed Maury.

"Then, of course, Madame, the neighbor, was just crazy with jealousy. 'I let Ice Mother ramble on, because her little boy's only got a jacket of ordinary ermine. But then her husband is such a rotten hunter. He can't catch anything but ermine in his traps and there's nothing commoner than ermine. If you're a really good hunter you're after arctic foxes and you use bows and arrows. Obviously, an arctic fox is something to be really proud of, something far more splendid than this wretched, commonplace ermine.' That's the way the conversations went on, no doubt. What the people said was very much the same sort of thing as they say today."

"Isn't it queer? Men always worry about the same things, whether it's today or any other time in history."

"That reminds me of what Goethe said," I added: " 'Mankind moves forward, but Man remains ever the same.' "

"Yes, yes," said Peyrony, "that really is so. Man remains the same; today he is what he was yesterday and thousands

Harpoon. La Laugerie Basse, Dordogne, France.

of years ago. Do you know, sometimes it seems to me that I'm actually living in the Ice Age, that I'm conversing with the men of those days. I feel as though they're no strangers, as though I know them. Here, in this rock-shelter, there lives a nice, friendly couple, husband and wife, but over there is a bad pair, a very bad pair indeed, always quarreling and fighting, while here there's song and laughter. Yes, I seem to be quite close to them, I can almost touch them . . . but . . . well, now you must come along to La Laugerie Haute. Take the mattock with you. We'll need it where we're going."

La Laugerie Haute lies quite near to La Laugerie Basse, and we walked along in the noontide sunlight beside the strange cliff-houses while Peyrony and Maury swapped reminiscences about Breuil, old Cartailhac, and Capitan— all renowned prehistorians who once excavated at these sites.

Then the ledge over the cliffs juts forward to form a great rock-shelter, an *abri sous roche,* overhanging a grotto. Here are more archaeological layers exposed in a most informative and useful way. More sticks bearing numbers. Peyrony was actually working on this site at the time of our visit, but things moved very slowly, for he had to excavate almost entirely alone and he did not progress more than a few inches a day.

He explained: "These are upper layers and, as at La Laugerie Basse, are exclusively Magdalenian. From these layers came the small art-objects found by Lartet and Christy about sixty* years ago. Later on, the site was worked by Massénat, Cartailhac, and many others. The objects recovered are all either in the British Museum or in the French National Museum of Antiquities at Saint-Germain near Paris. It was in 1863 that Lartet began to excavate here. He was lucky enough to light at once upon the Magdalenian layers and to discover art-objects which soon set the whole learned world in a turmoil. Nowadays we do not set out to discover art-objects. We are, of course, delighted if we do find any, but our main aim is to determine the sequence of strata, of layers. We want to know how the layers lie one upon the other, we want to find out what were the epochs when men lived here. Now, please look carefully at these upper strata. They are composed of several Magdalenian deposits or layers. Well, that's where the older investigators worked. I have now gone deeper down. Look and see how many strata underlie the Magdalenian. The whole site is now cut down to a depth of from three to four yards."

The excavation looked like a steep, sheer wall. We moved up right near to it, while Peyrony went on:

"Those who dug here before me thought that the Magdalenian layers rested on the bed-rock. It is easy to see how the mistake arose, because under the lowest Magdalenian

* I.e., from 1923, the date of the author's visit to the site. (*Translator's note.*)

stratum there comes a fairly thick sterile deposit. Even between the different Magdalenian layers, however, there occur sterile strata. Obviously, during the Magdalenian epoch (which lasted some thousands of years), the rock-shelter was uninhabited for long periods. Still, under the lowest Magdalenian I've found four Solutrean layers and then, lowest of all, Aurignacian strata.

Head of an animal, engraving on limestone. Mid-Magdalenian, La Laugerie Basse, Dordogne, France. Actual size.

"This succession of layers is to be discovered at almost all the sites in the region. For example, lately I've been digging at Le Ruth—that's not far from Le Moustier. There a middle Aurignacian stratum lies directly on the bed-rock, but after this stratum comes a sterile layer above which is an upper Aurignacian stratum which itself is covered by still another sterile layer. Then we get three Solutrean strata and right on the top there's the Magdalenian. So the order of succession is, from bottom upward, Aurignacian, Solutrean, Magdalenian."

I asked Peyrony whether at any site hereabouts the strata reached even farther back.

"Oh, yes, of course. Capitan and I, for instance, dug at La Ferrassie. There there's Mousterian under the Aurignacian and under the Mousterian there's Acheulian. But then again at La Ferrassie there's neither Solutrean nor Magdalenian."

He turned round and pointed to where Le Ruth and La Ferrassie lay. Then, with his finger, he indicated other places and sites, all within an easy distance of where we were, saying:

"There, I've not been able to do much digging but there's certainly Magdalenian.. There again I've ascertained the presence of Aurignacian while, there again, there's more Magdalenian."

I remarked that in that case every one of the rock-shelters must contain a prehistoric site.

"Oh, yes, you're absolutely right. This country was Ice Age Man's paradise. Just look well at this sunny, beautiful, sheltered valley. Notice how it just traps and holds the warmth, and that was all-important in the Ice Age, to find a home with a clement climate, or relatively clement. Even now the people who live here will never think of moving away . . . over there, now—you see where my finger's pointing?—well, that's where Professor MacCurdy of Yale University has been excavating over a number of years. He comes back every season and he always says that he never feels as well anywhere else as he does down here."

"That's good news. I mean about MacCurdy—he's the man who wrote the famous book, *Human Origins*. I'll have to go and see him—today if possible."

"Nothing's easier. He lives quite close to Les Eyzies. You'll find him at once. Everyone knows his house."

"Anyway, now let's get to work," put in Maury; "here's the mattock." Peyrony took leave of us. He wanted to visit some other sites.

We began to ply our mattocks. I kept somewhat to the left and he kept a little to the right.

"This is the Solutrean layer we're tackling; it's our present working-site."

Just after Peyrony had said that I turned up a typical laurel-leaf Solutrean blade.

"It's incredible how skillfully the Ice Age men worked. Just look at this: the surface is chipped on both sides, yet it is almost smooth."

"Yes, and marvelously thought out and accurately executed. Look how the piece lies in one's hand," said Maury.

I grasped the blade with thumb and forefinger. It really was like a laurel leaf.

Maury examined it.

"It's a remarkably fine specimen. Absolutely perfect; the points at both ends are admirably preserved."

We worked on. Soon Maury had a piece of bone, a spearhead bearing a little ornamentation.

"I'll tell MacCurdy you're here. He'll be pleased. It's now time for the midday rest. That must never be missed on any account. By the way, the food is excellent at Les Eyzies. Of course you know what is the speciality of the Périgord? Truffles. You'll have to try them while you're here. This is the truffle capital."

Laurel-leaf point: Solutrean II. From La Laugerie Haute, Dordogne, France.

It was not very far to Les Eyzies. Just a few turns in the road. But it had become very hot indeed. Noon bore down upon the highway. The stones were glowing and one could feel their heat through the soles of one's shoes. The meadows sloping to the Vézère's course seemed parched. The trees that had been so fresh in the early morning were now laden with dust.

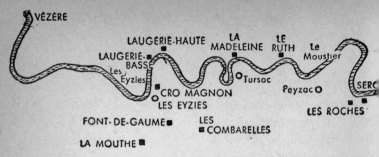

Sketch-map of Les Eyzies and surrounding country, Dordogne, France.

We found the truffles all right at the inn where the local red wine made everyone gay and good-humored.

A young Englishman sat at our table and, except for ourselves, he was the only customer. He told us his name. He was a Mr. Turner. I introduced myself: Kühn, Herbert Kühn.

"I think this is a most extraordinary country. When I was in Bordeaux I decided to come out here because I wanted to get some mountain scenery and mountain air, but here, though there are hills all right, no one pays any attention to them. Everyone's conversation is interlarded with words like 'Aurignacian,' 'Solutrean,' and 'Magdalenian.' People talk of these as though everyone ought to know what they mean. They point to a wall and say 'Magdalenian.' Perhaps you can tell me what that is. Ought one to know that sort of thing?"

"Oh, no, Mr. Turner, one really doesn't *have* to know: in fact, I'd say that most people have no idea at all of what these words mean. Still, of course, there are just two classes of people who do have to know. First of all the local inhabitants. Here every peasant and every little child—and there are lots of them, as I expect you've noticed—understands what's meant by 'Aurignacian,' 'Solutrean,' and 'Magdalenian.' Then, of course, there are the prehistorians.

There are not many of them, however, and they're pretty much scattered about all over the place. Anyway, if I may say so, you've come to the right shop, because as a matter of fact I am a prehistorian."

"Well, as you say, that's lucky. I was beginning to find this part of the world rather tiring. Now, please tell me what 'Magdalenian' is."

"First of all I must tell you that you've drifted into the Ice Age. Everything round about us here reminds us of the Ice Age. In fact the people hereabouts live on the Ice Age and they make a pretty good thing out of it."

"Ice Age—now that's what I call a pleasant subject of conversation when it's as hot as this. Still, it seems to me that the Ice Age has been over for some time past, eh?"

"No, no, not so very long, really. It ended about 10,000 years ago, but then this same (and last) Ice Age must have started several tens of thousands of years before that."

While I put another truffle on my plate, Mr. Turner drew me back gently but firmly to his question.

"But you were going to tell me what 'Magdalenian' is."

"Well, Magdalenian is the name given to the last phase, or period, of the Ice Age. During Magdalenian times the weather was beginning to get warmer. For instance, the mammoths, which earlier had flourished exceedingly in these parts, were almost extinct. But bisons and polar bears, reindeer and huge stags and wild horses wandered about over those hills back there. Cave bears lurked in the caverns and there were also wolverines, musk-oxen and even rhinoceroses."

"Rather a horrible picture."

"Maybe for us, but emphatically not for men of the Ice Age. Just think a minute. They had no manufactures, no agriculture, and they lived on animals. They needed the beasts. When the great creatures moved off northward toward the retreating glaciers, at the end of the Magdalenian period, that must have been a terrible catastrophe for the men who dwelt hereabouts."

"Well, well, so that's Magdalenian. And what do you find that dates from those times?"

"We find almost everything you can imagine; everything, that is, which the men of those days used and needed. Needles used for sewing skins, knives and blades employed in cutting, arrowheads, harpoons . . . in fact, the traps these men sprung, the bones they threw away at mealtimes, the charcoal they burned, the plants they gathered, the magic staves with which—before the hunt began —they exorcised or bewitched the game, and, above all, the marvelous paintings and engravings they executed."

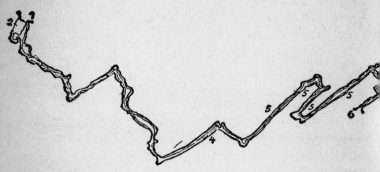

Ground plan of Les Combarelles Cave, near Les Eyzies, Dordogne, France: (1) Entrance. (2) Stable. (3) Engraved lines. (4) Beginning of the engravings. (5) Principal mass of engravings. (6) Descent to Lower Gallery and Pool.

"Pictures? You must be joking, Herr Kühn."

"Joking? Well, you'll see. I'll make a suggestion. Join up with us. Right after luncheon we're going to visit some of the pictures—big paintings and engravings, and all made by prehistoric men, many thousands of years ago. As a matter of fact, right here near Les Eyzies there are two famous prehistoric caverns: Font-de-Gaume and Les Combarelles. I've never seen them and I'm terribly impatient to view for myself these world-renowned late palaeolithic pictures. You'll have to admit it's astounding that we can gaze at, admire, examine pictures painted by men who lived, say,

Cave bear. Les Combarelles, Dordogne, France. Length 19 inches.

20,000 years ago, men who painted with regular oil colors such as we use nowadays. You'll find that the pictures are done with due regard for perspective and that they have depth and marked plastic quality. And those artists of far-off days used all sorts of colors ranging from yellow, through red, to brown and black."

At this point, the *patronne* brought in roast chicken and placed another flagon of wine upon the table.

"Well, I wanted to get away up into the mountains and take a good rest after all the hard work I put in before my examinations, and here I go again: I've got to learn something more. When I arrived I hadn't a care in the world, but all the time I've been here I've been in a continual state of surprise. There's something magic about this country. It's as though one had landed on the moon."

Thereupon he lit his pipe. Broad, deep wrinkles appeared upon his forehead as he blew great clouds of smoke out before him.

We sat for some time outside the inn and gazed across

Woolly mammoth. Les Combarelles, Dordogne, France. Length 28 inches.

meadows and valley. The heat of the day lay heavy upon the stones and the bright, light road was dazzling. Then we got up and made our way through the village toward the grotto of Les Combarelles.

Again the entrance lay through a dwelling where a peasant lived. His wife opened the door for us. We stepped in and through a side door got into the long, narrow, passage-like grotto. The woman took one lighted candle and her young daughter another. Turner and the two of us walked between the two Frenchwomen. At first, the long cave is fairly spacious, but it soon gets narrow, and then still narrower, until at last one must creep and crawl. Les Combarelles, in fact, is a very long and seemingly unending corridor or gallery. I am fairly big; so also was Mr. Turner. It was rather irksome for us to have to crouch down more and more as we advanced, but our guide was quite unmoved. Her hand pointed to the lines engraved upon the walls. At first we could not make out much. Then, however, a bear became quite clear and distinct. And after that we could see that the walls were covered with innumerable engravings and scratchings.

There is no painting at Les Combarelles, only drawing; that is, engraving. But it is amazing to remark how the lines and strokes are placed, how they stand out, how they leap along. The bear stumbles in clumsy fashion. Wearily he lifts one leg. . . . And there is a horse's head. Just a few lines, it's true, a few freely drawn strokes. There is no sort of well-defined outline drawing, but still the life, the movement, the expression are marvelous. There, again, is a high-maned wild horse, his neck stretched forward, his legs in rapid flight.

By this time the passage was very narrow and we managed to push forward with great difficulty. The candle flames flickered while great blobs of grease plopped to the ground. In a monotonous chant the woman declaimed: "Here the back, here the foot, here the head."

Often the animal is unrecognizable. All the engravings are

Les Combarelles, Dordogne, France. Dancing wizard pronouncing enchantments before the pictures.

relatively small, many no larger than a man's hand; others, however, are as long as one's forearm. Here is a mammoth, his powerful tusks curling upward and outward, the trunk drawn back against the body. Numerous bold strokes depict the beast's hairy coat. Slowly we accustom ourselves to a mass of lines, but many of the drawings cannot be comprehended at all. There, again, will be an animal standing out, quite clear and distinct and easily recognizable. And . . . there a dancing man.

We crept along still farther. A turn. Then another and still one more. Everywhere drawings, pictures. Then the passage began to slope downward. To the right, bisons, mammoths, reindeer. The woman kept on ahead of us. We knelt down and, while she held the light, followed the movements of her hand.

Les Combarelles, Dordogne, France. Head of a wolf: one-quarter actual size.

We had got to the point where the pictures cease. The passage, however, goes on, but it is not more than about twenty inches in height. We peered into the burrow while the woman told us of the depths into which the corridor plunges, of straight passages and of a subterranean lake at the very end. . . .

No more pictures. We turned round and crept our way out. Our knees pained us. The candle died down. On either side flickered once again reindeer, mammoths, bisons, lions . . . the grotto widened out. We could straighten up and walk forward erect. We were soon at the entrance. Once more through the cottage and we were in the warmth and sunlight of a fertile, gay, beaming dale. The foliage was fresh and young, the birds were twittering and the meadows were richly flecked with yellow blossoms. Over all the sun's glitter, while the earth seemed to laugh.

"Well, now, Mr. Turner, what do you think of the Ice Age?"

"I must confess I didn't expect anything like what we've seen—and in fact I didn't believe you when you talked about it. Are you sure it's all so old? Thousands of years? Then it's hard to imagine—here in the sunlight with everything green and warm and the heat burning up one's skin —it's hard to imagine that here, once upon a time, mammoths shambled along, polar bears and reindeer moved about."

We sat down in the grass. Mr. Turner pulled out his pipe again. Very slowly and pensively he filled it. As he blew out the first cloud of smoke into the sunlight, he looked at me and said:

"Well, Herr Kühn, you've proved to me today that the world is a more mysterious place than ever I thought."

III: Altamira

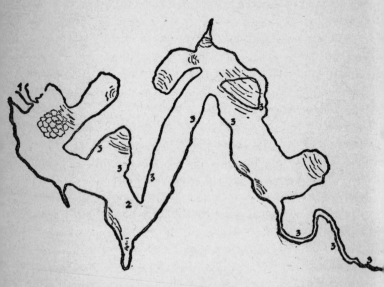

*Ground plan of the Altamira Cavern, near Santander, Spain:
(1) Existing entrance. (2) The Painted Ceiling. (3) Pictures.*

After we had made a short stay at San Sebastian, the
smartest seaside resort in Spain, we moved on to Santander and from there went to Torrelavega—quite close
to which place is Altamira, the finest of all the prehistoric
painted caverns, which was our goal. Torrelavega is a small
town but it holds something of the charm, and indeed the
magic, which are never far from one in Spain. We had in
our possession a letter from the Abbé Breuil—who was the
first to study the Altamira pictures—addressed to Alcalde
del Rio, the mayor of Torrelavega.

In the main street we asked a man to show us the way, which after all was not difficult to find, for the street was not very long. In a few minutes we had discovered the mayor's dwelling and had been ushered into his living-room. It was quite empty save for rows of chairs drawn up against the walls. Then Alcalde del Rio came in. He was a small, lively man speaking no language but his native Spanish, but he greeted us with a torrent of words and his eyes beamed as he took Breuil's letter into his hand.

"Now what would you like to see? Altamira, of course, but perhaps something else too?"

"Yes, indeed, a great deal more if it's possible: La Pasiega, Covalanas, Pindal, El Castillo and even still more of the Cantabrian caverns."

"Well, I quite understand that but I must tell you quite frankly that it's not going to be easy to see all the caves you mention. You'd not be able to find your way alone, and who's going to act as guide? I can't think of anyone who knows the caverns except shepherds and local peasants, but you'd not be able to come in contact with them. So what can we do?"

"Haven't you got any acquaintances who'd come along with us; say, maybe, an office-boy or one of your official subordinates?"

"Hm . . . well, anyway, you'll be able to see Altamira alone, it's not too difficult and that'll be one thing at any rate. You can hire a car here to take you out to Altamira. But it's quite out of the question for you to try to find the other sites alone, and I can't for the life of me think of any-one to show you the way. Let me think . . . well, after all, perhaps, at a pinch, you might be able to get to Pindal by yourselves. I'll write you out an itinerary. It's like this: first of all you go to Colombres and then farther on to Pimiango and there you'll, no doubt, discover someone who'll show you the way . . . but it really is quite impossible for you to attempt La Pasiega without a guide. In fact, it's all so complicated that I'm not at all certain that I could find the way myself. It's so many years since I was there and the scrub and bushes grow so fast and change the entire appearance of the ground. . . . All the same, we could take in La Pasiega the same day as El Castillo. In fact, the two caverns are fairly close together."

"You don't really mean that you're willing to devote a whole day to showing us around?"

"Yes, indeed, I'll be delighted to. What made me hesitate a little was that I'm very busy just now with inspections, but if you'd like to go out to Altamira tomorrow, then we can all three go to El Castillo and La Pasiega the day after. You're the first German scientists ever to come here and I am very pleased at the idea of taking you round the caverns. . . . You know of course that, as a matter of fact, I found most of them myself?"

"Yes, I do know, naturally; we all realize that you have rendered very valuable services to the whole discipline and science of prehistory."

"It's very possible that, without my aid and assistance, Breuil and Obermaier would not have been able to do what they did. I used to help them quite a lot in their work. And, perhaps, what you don't know"—here his eyes darted brightly—"is that I, too, have published a book on Altamira?"

"Oh, yes, we do . . . it appeared in the same year as the big volume by Breuil and Obermaier, and that bears your name as well as that of the other two scientists."

"Well, I'm very glad you know about it, very glad indeed . . . but have you got a copy of my book?"

"No," I said, "unfortunately I haven't; it's rather difficult to come by, but I've read it, I got it out of the library in Paris."

"Then I'll give you a copy."

He disappeared but soon returned with a volume bearing the title *Las Pinturas y Grabados de las Cavernas prehistóricas de la Provincia de Santander;* that is to say, *The*

Paintings and Engravings in the Prehistoric Caves of the Province of Santander, published at Santander in 1906.

"I'm very grateful to you indeed for this, it's most kind of you." We shook hands warmly.

"Now you must tell me all about Breuil," he said. "I have a great admiration for him, you know; he's a most distinguished man of science, a learned man such as you don't find many of nowadays, and then he's so modest, so natural. . . ."

"We met a few weeks ago in Paris. We lunched together several times and became very good friends. His lively manner when he talks—or writes—is most attractive and his bright, shrewd eyes make a lasting impression."

"Oh, yes, he's always full of life, full of energy. I well remember how he never used to get tired during the excavations and explorations. It was never too much for him to clamber about up in the high hills and mountains or to scramble through thickets and bushes. And one can't say too often that these expeditions are generally very tiring indeed, sometimes almost unbearably so. After all, these Cantabrian Mountains are just a part of the Pyrenees, a prolongation of the Pyrenean Chain. Our northern Spanish ranges peak up into lofty summits and the whole Cantabrian mass forms a high barrier where the weather is often raw and cold, or, when the wind changes—not seldom without any warning at all—it becomes intolerably hot. It's this rapid transition that's so very trying. And then again it rains all the time. It rains here in these regions more than in any other part of Europe. We'll be visiting some places —Pimiango for instance—where the people always go about on 'stilts,' one might say; or, anyway, they wear clogs with three bits of wood attached so that their feet are kept dry. As a matter of fact, in that particular spot round about Pimiango it is very rare indeed to come across a day when it does not rain. The ground is always sodden and wet. You see, it's like this. On the northern face of the mountains the raw winds from the Bay of Biscay blow almost continuously, whereas, from the south, from over the tablelands of Castile, come the warm wind-currents . . . obviously there must be rain all the time. Despite what people generally imagine, Spain's not a country like Italy with a warm, equable climate. Spain presents all sorts of variations. If Andalusia is a paradise with a climate like that of North Africa, in the Castiles it's often harsh and chilly—in winter sometimes as cold as in Germany—while in Asturias and Galicia it is damp and rainy all the year round, in fact it's more like Norway than Africa! And it's just in this wet region that we've got to travel.

"Breuil and Obermaier and I thoroughly explored this whole area: we clambered about from peak to peak, from mount to mount. We followed tracks known only to shepherds and peasants. Often, very often, we found no caves at all. What our guides, in perfect good faith, had pointed out to us as being caverns were just superficial depressions in the rock-face. Yet we had to follow every clue, we had to explore, to examine everything that looked in the least promising. You see, it's like this. In a general way, the local inhabitants won't themselves venture into the caves at all. That's where the spirits have their abode. Sometimes, indeed, you can't get anyone to accompany you even as far as the entrance. Mind you, I'm not complaining, this is all to the good. If there wasn't this sort of taboo, the pictures in the caverns would have been long since destroyed. Not one would have survived to our day."

"But how did you first come to get interested in archaeology and prehistory? Did you go in for these things when you were quite young?"

"No, not at all," replied Alcalde del Rio. "First of all I must tell you that I'm not what we call here in Spain a 'professional' mayor. With us, mayors are elected for a few years, then, after serving their term, they take up their old jobs again. I am a schoolmaster, but I've always been interested in problems concerning the origin and early history

of man. I had read a great many books, but I had had no
practical experience of archaeology, I had not had my imagination really excited. Then, one day back in 1903, I got
to hear that two French scientists had arrived at Altamira
and that they were going to dig there and study the paintings on the cave walls. So I made my way to Altamira,
introduced myself, and was received in very friendly fashion. Cartailhac, at this time, was already an old gentleman.
He held a chair at Toulouse University and was a very
charming, delightful, and distinguished personage. Breuil, in
1903, however, was quite young, not more than twenty-six
years of age. Prehistorian and priest, he was, as far as prehistory went, a disciple of Cartailhac. But Breuil was the
man who, after the world had forgotten about it, again
drew attention to the wonders of Altamira."

"So, as a matter of fact, you lived right through much of
the history of the famous discoveries. In fact, you knew at
first hand the heroic age of exploration and research in late
palaeolithic prehistory."

"Oh, yes, that's true enough, and I'm proud of it, too.
Those were the finest years of my life. . . . As a matter of
fact, I must say that I discovered some of the caverns when
I was quite alone. Take for instance the case of El Castillo
in 1903. I was the first man—since the end of the last Ice
Age—to walk through the chambers and halls of that
grotto. In the same way—though in some instances accompanied by Father Sierra from Limpias, who was as keen as
myself—I was the first to enter the caverns of Covalanas,
La Haza, Salitre and Hornos de la Peña. Sierra and I found
all four during the months of July, August, and September,
1903. And all four are adorned with prehistoric pictures.
These caves are all here in the province of Santander. You
ought to have seen how excited we were, and how trium-
phant, when we discovered more new paintings and pictures. We used to fall on each other's necks and embrace
. . . just imagine . . . Covalanas, now, that's got most
lovely and lively pictures. At La Haza are eight figures of

horses. Salitre contains four pictures . . . that we saw at first. Then there are a few others I discovered on later visits. But Hornos de la Peña was the most magnificent. There you can distinguish no less than thirty-four pictures, some of which are really remarkably beautiful.

"Later on, Obermaier and a Frenchman called Bouyssonie did some digging in Hornos de la Peña. And they found something of quite peculiar importance for the dating of the pictures. What these two men discovered was a sketching-block that had been used to make the small-scale drawings which later were to be reproduced on a large scale on the cave's walls. At the entrance to the grotto, and on a block of stone, are sketches of horses. Only the outlines are shown. Now, just imagine, Obermaier found the 'original' sketch of these pictures and he found it in an upper Aurignacian layer. In point of fact only the hind part of the beast was preserved engraved upon a piece of horse-bone. The other part had been broken off and lost. But the sketch and the rock-picture are exactly alike. So, owing to this sketch, the picture can be with certainty dated to a late phase of Aurignacian culture.

"Still, I think that the most important discovery was made at El Castillo near Puente Viesgo. I found this cavern myself, alone on a very bad, rainy day. I'll never forget the date. It was November 8, 1903. At that time the entrance was so low that it could hardly be noticed. It was just a small hole in the ground. Nowadays, as you'll see, the entrance is over sixty feet high. It's an enormous, gaping aperture. And that just goes to show how much debris and rubbish had accumulated in the course of millennia. All the culture phases are represented, from Magdalenian through Azilian to Neolithic. The Magdalenian stratum is particularly rich and important. Under this, again, come first of all a Solutrean and then three Aurignacian layers. Each one of them is sandwiched in between sterile strata. But there is also lower palaeolithic because two still lower layers were prospected. One is Mousterian and the other Acheulian."

"So," I commented, "it seems to me that El Castillo is one of the very few sites where all the culture phases are represented by strata occurring in what may be called their 'standard' or 'classical' sequence and position. In fact the collection goes right down to Chellean-Abbevillian. Is there any other site where all the strata are so clearly exposed? I don't know of any. What a pity it is that there's still no special publication entirely devoted to this most significant cave of El Castillo."

"My experience," answered Alcalde del Rio, "is confined to the caverns of this, our Cantabrian region. But these I do know well enough; very well, in fact. I also know of many pictures which are not reproduced in the big, well-known volumes devoted to the Cantabrian caverns."

At this juncture, our host's wife came into the room. She was a sprightly lady clad entirely in black, as is the custom hereabouts. The master of the house presented us and told her that we had come to Torrelavega because we were interested in prehistoric caves and their pictures. She shook hands with us and then left the room, to return a few minutes later carrying fruit, plates, glasses, and a flask of wine.

"Well, then, that's what we'll do. We'll go off tomorrow morning to Altamira. Let's all meet, at say eight o'clock, at the Torrelavega hotel for dinner. Perhaps Señora Alcalde del Rio and you will give us the pleasure of being our guests. And then we can discuss plans for the day after tomorrow."

Our host agreed and we left his house delighted to have found someone so friendly and helpful. On our way back to the hotel we called at the garage he had mentioned and ordered a car for the following day.

It was still cool, in fact it was quite cold, when we got into the car the next morning; but, then, it was very early. We took along with us a camera and a good supply of drawing-paper, water colors, and paint brushes.

It was not long before Torrelavega was far behind us and we were climbing up steeply into the mountains. Then the sun's rays broke through the clouds and the landscape lit up under the radiance of morning. Bare hills. No trees. Rocky heights. Beasts grazing while their herdsmen stood still watching us drive by. We dashed through a small village. Women were doing their shopping in the market. A man clad all in somber black walked past with solemn and measured tread.

We soon got to Santillana del Mar, the town where Altamira's discoverer, Don Marcelino de Sautuola, had his country house and the property that is still in the possession of his family. Don Marcelino was, of course, no longer living at the time of our visit, but his daughter, a venerable old lady, still resided in the castle. She it was who, at the age of five, was the real discoverer of the prehistoric frescoes of Altamira.

Santillana is quite a small place and the castle is one of the most prominent features of the town. The entrance to the property is through a baroque entrance-gate which affords a view of the mansion surrounded by trees. The house itself is not very large but is a charming example of Spanish sixteenth-century architecture.

We stopped the car in order to admire the whole assemblage. Meanwhile the driver had fetched the key to the cave and we set off again. The road led through meadows and fields, for the countryside was now quite level and flat. The car stopped at a place that looked a long way away from everywhere. We had arrived at the cavern.

We would never have thought that this was the entrance to the world-renowned cave of Altamira, the most beautiful and the most spacious of all the prehistoric painted caverns of Ice Age times. As a matter of fact, when we speak of "caverns" we nearly always think of cliffs, gorges, hills, peaks and canyons. But a cavern in a flat meadow; that is something that strikes us as very curious indeed.

A small stone monument stood near the entrance—and that was all. It was a considerable time after our visit that

the entrance was enlarged and the little museum built. As it
was, we went down a slope from the flat meadow right into
the earth. There was a low approach and then there we
were standing before an iron door. The chauffeur unlocked
it and pushed it open. We lighted up our acetylene lamps
and, after a few steps forward, found ourselves in the Great
Hall. First of all one's eyes have to get accustomed to the
darkness and the dim lights. Then, slowly, one begins to
find one's bearings.

A huge cavern under a shallow vaulted roof set with
many protuberances. The floor slopes obliquely upwards.
The first thing we could see was, quite near the entrance,
and written in candle-black, the name "Alfonso XII."

"And where are the pictures?" we asked. The chauffeur
pointed to the ceiling. Then, suddenly, we beheld the mass
of paintings. Those bosses, protuberances, and humps took
on movement and life. One of the lumps carried the figure
of a standing bison, another swelling bore a beast all hud-
dled up. The prehistoric artist utilized the irregularities of
the surface in order to convey the impression of relief. In
fact these frescoes are paintings and sculptures at one and
the same time. Or, let us say, rather they are paintings in
relief. Because of this peculiar character it is quite impossible to give a good reproduction—on paper anyway—of the
entire assemblage. Here, for instance, is a hind. The picture
measures about four and a half feet long. It is masterly in
drawing, design, execution, and painting. There, again, is a
bison shown struck with a spear. It is nothing short of astounding to observe how the beast has sunk its head, how
the hind legs double up, how the coat shines like that of a
living animal, how the figure stands out, how the painting
shows relief and displays remarkable plastic quality, and
how the colors are applied despite all the difficulties presented by the surface. It is a thing one can never forget
once one has seen it. It is miraculous when one reflects that
the painting is at least ten thousand years old—and may

well be more ancient—that it is among the most venerable upon this earth and was executed millennia before Mesopotamia, Egypt, or China existed.

Then that wild boar over there. It looks as natural as though it were a living thing and had been cast upon this ceiling by some magic. The color sparkles, almost heaves . . . these are living pictures, the image of life itself. These are animals, painted in the flash of movement, as close as may be to reality, to actual presence. These are pictures that are visions of everyday life. As shown in their art, prehistoric men seem very near to us, familiar. There is nothing of the stiffness, the pomposity, the aloofness of the classical arts of Mesopotamia and Egypt. Most of us have some sort of idea that early art, art in its beginnings, must be, or perhaps should be, hieratic, solemn, harsh . . . then we are confronted with the wonders of Altamira and with paintings that are quite natural, that are immediate to our consciousness.

We stood and stared and stared, quite overwhelmed. Through my mind ran the memories of the most magnificent and sublime things I had ever beheld—all pell-mell they came rushing back to me: the Sistine Chapel, Mona Lisa, the Sistine Madonna, the moving portrait of Rembrandt as an old man at The Hague, things by Titian, by Fra Angelico, the most significant works that I had beheld of the great Chinese and Japanese masters. In my imagination some of the greatest pictures floated before my eyes. Peaks of man's achievement, supreme moments of artistic creation. And the pictures seen upon the rocks of Altamira belong indubitably to the most significant and important of man's creations.

It is not only the frescoes' stupendous age. It is not just the thought that they date from palaeolithic times—an epoch so distant from us that we can hardly imagine it. It is not only the setting, right upon the fringes of man's ancient settlement. It is not that the paintings were created before history, before writing, before records. It is just the pictures, for themselves alone and by themselves. They are in form, color, and execution among the finest and most precious works of art upon this earth.

The Altamira paintings have their own individual style, their own peculiar rhythm, their own sort of construction. And they exhibit an art in which there is complete mastery of form. In fact, these pictures bear the stamp of sovereign creation. The artist's purpose is wholly reflected in his art. His plan is carried out with complete success. Thus the beholder is enthralled—and satisfied.

But even if the Altamira paintings were as stiff and formal as those of Egypt, Mesopotamia, or Byzantium, they might, of course, be in their own way quite perfect. We are able to appreciate the quality of wholly alien art styles, say those of Mexico or Peru, or even China and Japan. But it is not the style alone that so powerfully appeals to us. It is something which transcends art conventions and age. It is quality. Of course, even in Old Stone Age—that is, Ice Age—times there were good and bad pictures, significant and insignificant paintings and sculptures. But on the Bison Ceiling at Altamira we behold masterpieces in every meaning of the word.

We drew nearer to the pictures and examined the colors. Formerly the cave's floor was not cut down as it is now—after Obermaier's extensive excavations—and no path had been made for the visitor. So, at the time when we visited Altamira, one could still touch the pictures. Very carefully and gingerly I laid a finger lightly upon the color-surface and felt it was damp, as though fresh. The pigment was laid on thick, much thicker, in fact, than is usual in the case of modern paintings. I dabbed the smear of color onto a piece of paper and could see that it was deep red, much more brilliant, indeed, in tone than one would have imagined— from looking at the frescoes—that it would prove to be. Hardly any of the reproductions I have seen convey anything of this freshness, of this depth of coloring. As it is, the red is vivid red and the black is deepest black. As a matter of fact, judging from the state of the pigment alone, it would not be hard to imagine that the frescoes were executed but yesterday. The doubts which were long entertained concerning the authenticity of the pictures are easy enough to understand.

The solution of the riddle lies in the special conditions which obtained in the cavern. It was, of course, hermetically sealed up. The entrance through which we came was excavated only a comparatively few years ago. The ancient entrance lay far away—at the end of the Long Gallery. And this was blocked up as slabs and bits of rock fell down from the roof—probably in Ice Age times. Thus it came

Wall painting in late Magdalenian style. One-tenth actual size. Altamira, near Torrelavega, Province of Santander, Spain.

about that since upper palaeolithic days no man had gazed upon the pictures. No breath of air blew upon them while the temperature remained absolutely equable and constant throughout the millennia. The cavern, indeed, would have remained forever hidden had not a fox made its earth in the meadow and if a dog had not been sent by a hunter to look for the fox. The dog found the earth all right, disappeared into it and did not come back. So the hunter began to dig for his animal and, as he dug, he lighted upon the cavern of Altamira.

All this happened in the year 1868, and not until then had any outside air touched the pictures nor had any human being entered the grotto.

We sat down upon a large stone and gazed toward the

pictures. Here the Ice Age artist must have stood; here mixed his colors before laying them with a brush upon the rock walls. That delicate line, maybe, he drew with his fingers. Nowhere does the outline dominate. In no place is the outline the decisive feature. Everything was conceived and was displayed as though originating from the interior of the forms themselves. The painting was so executed that the figures were to be pictorial. The drawing, the linear aspect, was not a main preoccupation of the artist.

I fell to wondering with what style of modern art the Altamira pictures could be usefully compared, and, as far as I could see, then and now, it is only with the work of the nineteenth- and early twentieth-century Impressionists. The Impressionists tackled comparable problems and sought to solve them by subordinating line to color, problems of how to convey the impression of depth and space, of the vivid and momentary play of light, in fact, of how to present movement as it is seen and seized in an instantaneous glance.

That wild boar is running. We see him in a flash. This bison is crumpling up and the artist was able to reproduce the beast's every movement and in telling fashion. He was not, indeed, mainly concerned with presenting what was of the essence, of the nature of the creature's permanent being, so to speak. In fact, the artist's principal task, his aim and object, were not those of almost all of what we call archaic art. On the contrary, prehistoric art, the prehistoric art we see before us at Altamira, is concerned with the fleeting moment, with what exists here and now. It is just such an attitude which makes this age-old art so close to us, makes it seem contemporary and nearly allied to our own. I have often felt, when admiring well-known works of art from Egypt, Mesopotamia, and Byzantium, and even those of Romanesque times and traditions, that such things are essentially alien to us. Now, I realized that they were, indeed, farther away from us in spirit and in execution than the prehistoric paintings in the northern Spanish caverns.

Of course these "classical" things produce a deep impression, their impact is powerful and lasting, but they lack a quality which one can only call "momentary," this cutting or slicing of the moment out of the whole action, this vivid flash by which the whole depth and force of content is concentrated into a second of time.

First we sat on one block of stone and then we moved to another, but wherever we were the pictures spoke aloud as the witnesses of ages long since passed away. I could not help reflecting that in the days when the prehistoric artists were working at the adorning of the caverns, out there—on the leas where our car was waiting while shepherds tended their sheep—bisons, mammoths, and reindeer roamed . . . the Pyrenean glaciers came right down almost to the cave's entrance.

I have said that the prehistoric artists "adorned" the cavern, but, in fact, the term is hardly apt. The Altamira paintings do not really adorn the ceiling. They bear no direct relation at all to the great span of the vault. It is true that here and there bosses and bumps were utilized, but the ceiling itself is not, as it were, organized, articulated, or interpreted by the paintings. Each individual beast exists for itself alone. The figures are all mixed up, pell-mell; some, even, cover others. Obviously there was no thought-out plan. One picture is just here . . . and, well, another is there. It seems clear that at no moment had the adornment of the vault, as such, been an object of the artist. At no time was his vision directed toward unity, composition. What he wanted was an individual animal, but he wanted it as it is seen in nature, seen in the moment of haste, of falling, of death. Art, for itself, was doubtless a preoccupation of the painter or else he would hardly have exercised so much care and taken so much trouble, have expended so much of his spiritual strength upon the work. But some other aim and object was certainly bound up with that of art for its own sake. And those aims and objects we call Rite, Magic, Religion.

In prehistoric times, just as with the Greeks or in our own Middle Ages, art and religion were closely allied.

In such caverns as Altamira wild beasts were bewitched; here danced the magicians and the other members of the tribe. Here were the pictures conjured, shot at—either in mimicry or with real weapons. Such subterranean halls and chambers were shrines of art and of religion comparable to our Sistine Chapel or to the Madonna dell'Arena shrine that contains Giotto's frescoes in Padua.

I walked about and then sat down here and there. I wanted to seize this wonder, to grasp it with my hands, so that I might never forget it, never allow it to fade away from me. This was for me a most blessed day. I had been privileged to approach Altamira. My dream had been realized, my long-deferred hope fulfilled.

Wall paintings in late Magdalenian style. One-tenth actual size. Altamira, near Torrelavega, Province of Santander, Spain.

Then I set to work to draw, to paint, to reproduce the colors, as far as I could, in their strength and brilliance. The hours slipped by. At noon we picnicked upon the leas and drank the pleasing Spanish wine we had brought with us.

Afterwards we explored the farther gallery. Here also, on all sides, were more, and then more, pictures. An extraordinarily lifelike engraving of a stag . . . then drawings depicting the wizards themselves, men with beasts' masks . . . small sketches no larger than a man's hand. And I copied what most struck my imagination and what most appealed to me. And all the while, the precious hours spilled away. In these ever gloomy halls you are plunged into a timeless universe. You are out of our world. You are set among other ages. You are upon another planet.

When, at last, we did leave the cavern, it was late afternoon.

Once we were settled into the car we felt tired out and quite exhausted. In Santillana del Mar we pulled up again while the driver got down to give back the key. When he reappeared he was accompanied by a servant who asked us if we would be pleased to take tea with the lady of the castle upon her terrace.

The mistress of the domain was elderly, dressed all in black, and of most charming appearance and manner.

"What sort of an impression did Altamira make on you?" she said as she held out her hand in greeting.

"Señora, we are completely fascinated. We are enchanted, we are under the spell of what we have seen."

"Yes, it's astounding, isn't it? I've seen the frescoes, it may be, well, a thousand times in the course of my life, and on every occasion they gripped me as though I was beholding them for the first time. And yet, it's hard to say wherein lies their magic. I think it is in a combination of circumstances, the darkness of the grottoes, the mystery surrounding the pictures, their incredible age and, then, of course, there is the really superb painting."

"No doubt you are right. That must be it. I've seen a good many of the world's wonders but none of them affected me as the Altamira pictures have. And, señora, we are very grateful to you that you who discovered the pictures are kind enough to receive us as guests in your house."

"Well, at least, I think we may say that I shall be forever known as the very youngest person ever to have discovered Ice Age paintings and pictures."

"Oh, there's no doubt whatever about that. You yourself lived all through the romance of discovery, and, as you are the only person fitted to talk about it, won't you please tell us how it all happened?"

"Yes, I'd be delighted to. Altamira was the greatest adventure of my life . . . and, also, my bitterest disappointment. The story begins with the 1878 Paris International Exhibition and my father's visit to it. Among all the wonders of the great show nothing made a more profound impression upon my father than the prehistoric artifacts discovered by Piette in the Dordogne department of France. These tools and instruments, as you know, furnished abundant proof that man had existed at the same time as animals now extinct in Western Europe; that is to say, mammoths, musk-oxen, bisons, and reindeer. However, by no means everyone accepted the proof; the evidence was, indeed, hotly and fiercely contested. Nevertheless, Piette really was able to produce drawings and engravings dating from these prehistoric times, drawings, indeed, executed by prehistoric man who lived countless ages farther back than was then generally believed possible. My father became very excited about the whole business. Again and again he went back to view the glass cases and to gaze upon the implements and art objects.

"One day my father met Piette himself and during their conversation my father asked Piette about caverns, artifacts, excavation methods, and a thousand and one other things to do with field work in archaeological research.

"When he got back to Santillana my father went out to the Altamira cavern, in fact he spent much time there. He would take a spade with him and try to excavate. His great dream was to turn up artifacts comparable with those Piette had discovered in the Dordogne. One day—it was in November, 1879—my father got back from the cave and his hands were full of stone and bone implements. Of course, I had no idea what all these things might mean, but judging from my father's excitement I felt that something most unusual must have occurred. After that he worked and dug, out at Altamira, almost every day, and once he took me with him. I was just five years old. While I was running about in the cavern and playing about here and there, suddenly I made out forms and figures on the roof. I pointed the pictures out to my father, but he just laughed. But soon, however, he got more interested, held his lamp aloft while he made out a picture here and a picture there. He dabbed at the color with his fingers and recognized that the pigments were real 'oil colors,' that is to say they had been mixed with a fatty medium. He was so enthusiastic that he could hardly speak.

"Yes, I can see the whole scene quite clearly now. At my age one tends to forget a good deal but I have never forgotten any detail of what happened that day at Altamira. On our way back to the house we did not speak. Later on, my father often told me what had been in his mind as we were going back to Santillana. . . . The cavern had been discovered some ten years before by a local sportsman. The paintings, then, could not possibly be modern, since if, for any reason, an artist had been at work in the cave my father would surely have heard of it. Our part of the world here is so isolated that we know of every stranger who passes by. Moreover, since any artists would have had to bring with them considerable quantities of materials, it was quite out of the question that they could have done any painting at Altamira without everyone knowing about it. Moreover, even supposing for a moment that it had been possible for modern artists to paint the pictures, what could have been the aim and object of portraying extinct beasts upon the roof of an out-of-the-way cavern in a remote part of Spain? But, on the other hand, the pictures were of such superb quality and of such consummate execution that it was difficult to imagine that they could have been the work of prehistoric men. Still, all the same, no other explanation seemed possible. Moreover, as he came to think of it, my father remembered that, years before, he had noticed some black lines upon the cave walls, but at the time he paid no attention to them and attached no importance to their existence.

"The first thing my father did after the discovery was to write a letter to Professor Vilanova in Madrid. In those days he was the most celebrated geologist in all Spain. Very soon after he got my father's letter the professor came here to visit us. He himself did some digging in the cave, found some artifacts, turned up a few cave-bear bones . . . and saw the paintings. He, too, was compelled to agree that these could not be anything else but prehistoric.

"Then he and my father went to Santander where Vilanova gave a lecture at which he declared that the Altamira frescoes were undoubtedly of late palaeolithic date. This pronouncement caused, as you may well imagine, a great deal of excitement. The newspapers carried front-page articles headed 'The Prehistoric Paintings at Altamira near Santander.' Press photographers began to arrive here. Illustrations appeared in the big Madrid dailies. The throng of visitors was tremendous and our little village began to look like a popular pilgrimage-place. We had people staying in the house all the time and I was very proud because my father always roundly declared that I was the discoverer of the pictures and that I had been the first person to see them. So there appeared also pictures of me in the papers and you may imagine how important I felt.

"Excitement, however, reached its peak when the King himself came to see the paintings. He stayed with us and I was presented to him. Just think of it. The King! The servant who accompanied the sovereign, his suite, and my father into the cave used the candle which he held in order to trace, in candle-smoke, the words 'Alfonso XII.' I can remember that wonderful day as though it were yesterday. I can see the King now and recall his look as he stood opposite me and said:

"'So you're the famous discoverer of the pictures?' And this aloud in the presence of everyone. Can you realize what that meant for a Spaniard—for any Spaniard? And how much more for me, a small child?

"About this time my father wrote a little book about the Altamira pictures and the stream of visitors became ever greater. Alas! suddenly, all this wonderful period came to an end. It had been all a dream. Everything was forgotten. Altamira lay deserted and no more guests came to our house.

"And this was the reason. The scientists of the day unanimously refused to accept the pictures as prehistoric. Without any exception they all agreed that the whole thing was a hoax perpetrated just in order to fool the scientists.

"In 1880 the Congress of Prehistoric Archaeology met in Lisbon. Prehistorians and archaeologists from all over the world took part in the meetings—Virchow from Germany, Lubbock from England, Cartailhac from France, Pigorini from Italy, Undset from Norway (he was the father of the novelist Sigrid Undset), Montelius from Sweden, and Ribeiro from Portugal. A great gathering of learned men. On the agenda of the Congress figured a proposed expedition to Altamira. Vilanova had made all the preparations. But no one came. Drawings of the pictures had been exhibited in the halls of the Congress. These reproductions had been the subject of much discussion and debate, the upshot of which was that everyone agreed in rejecting the Altamira frescoes. Nothing was known which could be compared with them. The sad fact was that they had made their appearance too soon. Scientific opinion, at least, was not prepared for them.

"You can imagine what a blow all this was for my father. He felt that the hostile articles were aimed directly at him.

And anti-Altamira articles now began to appear in the public press as well as in the scientific reviews. Though much discouraged, my father did make just one more attempt to vindicate the authenticity of the paintings. He attended the French Congress that met at Algiers in 1882, but his efforts were in vain. In the year that the International Congress held its session in Berlin, my father submitted his book and a report to the Congress, but no discussion on Altamira was allowed, or at any rate took place. Finally, even Vilanova deserted us. When, in 1889, the International Congress met in Paris, the name of Altamira was not even pronounced. Silence fell all about us here.

"It was twenty-three years later before Altamira woke to life again. And it was two French archaeologists who were responsible for the revival. They were Cartailhac, formerly one of the most prominent of the skeptics, and a much younger man, Breuil, Cartailhac's disciple in prehistory. In their own land they had discovered painted caverns and among them were caves filled with layers of deposits which hid some of the pictures so that these became visible only when the deposits had been removed. It was, therefore, quite clear that such pictures dated from prehistoric times. Among grottoes containing such drawings and paintings were La Mouthe near Les Eyzies and Pair-non-Pair in the Gironde department.

"But what was really decisive and most important was the discovery in 1901 both of Font-de-Gaume and Les Combarelles near Les Eyzies—"

"We've just been visiting both of those caverns."

"Yes, you've mentioned that. Well, in that case you can compare. Which do you think is the more impressive: Font-de-Gaume or Altamira?"

"Oh, Altamira without any question. In Font-de-Gaume the colors have long since lost their freshness, whereas at Altamira you've got the impression that you're looking at pictures executed quite recently."

"Well, that was what Cartailhac and Breuil thought in

1903. You ought to have seen the two of them when they had been working here some time. They were enthralled, and kept saying they were living in another world, in a dream, a fairy story. They used to sit out here on this terrace after their day's work and talk about copying the pictures, about their excavations and about the new discoveries they made almost every day. Alcalde del Rio joined forces with them, and I can well recollect when he found the slab of stone engraved with the representation of a hind. The piece lay embedded in an early Magdalenian stratum, and, just imagine it . . . the same picture, exactly the same picture, is to be found on the walls of the Altamira gallery—only on a larger scale, of course—a big mural picture showing greater detail than the small sketch. So the stone was the sketching-block, the trial-piece, so to speak. You can imagine how much discussion this gave rise to, for it had become quite clear that men of the Old Stone Age had schools where drawing-lessons were given and where painting was taught. Artists must have really been through a long training before they ventured to try their hand on the execution of the large murals."

"That's undoubtedly right," I said, "there have been other discoveries of trial-pieces. For a long time now the Altamira sketch has not been the only one in existence. There is also one at Font-de-Gaume. The mural, the figure of a gigantic old bison with most powerfully developed withers—it's a quite exceptionally outstanding picture—has been known since 1903. Twenty-three years later, that is to say in 1926, the sketch for the Font-de-Gaume bison turned up in a rock-shelter known as the Abri de la Genière, near Serrières-sur-Ain in the Ain department of France . . . and that's at least a hundred and eighty miles away from Font-de-Gaume. It looks, therefore, very much as though in prehistoric times men, when it was possible, must have not only prized but preserved sketch-blocks with trial-pieces and perhaps traded in them. Of course, we can't be sure of that, but art was clearly held in great esteem and it is certain that fine achievement, execution, and artistry were recognized and highly appreciated."

The sun was now sinking behind the trees of the park. The light got thinner, paler, dimmer. We took our leave of the old lady and made our way back to Torrelavega.

In the car we sat silent and gazed out onto the country-side. In its relief, and indeed in its general appearance, it has not altered very much in the last, let's say, thirty thousand years, but the great cold has lifted while the living creatures that once flourished here are no more—the beasts, the herds, the men. . . .

But one thing lives on, the spiritual act whereby wizards, shamans, magicians, using the mingled elements of religion and art, performed their creative operation. The spirit is more than the flesh and links us of today with our remote, far-off ancestors of prehistoric times. The pictures left by men of the Ice Age act as powerfully—though possibly in a different way—upon us as they did upon the men of ten thousand years ago, and as long as such art exists it will not fail to enthrall those who look upon it.

For art is creation; that is to say, the artist is a god in that he can make, can create, like a god.

IV: El Castillo

Ground plan of El Castillo Cavern, near Puente Viesgo, Province of Santander, Spain: (1) Entrance. (2) The Frieze of Hands. (3) Paintings of hands. (4) Tectiform signs. (5) Paintings in black pigment. (6) Polychrome paintings. (7) Engravings.

We were sitting on a bench outside the Puente Viesgo Inn high up in the Cantabrian Mountains. There were first of all the innkeeper, then Alcalde del Rio, Rita, and I. The weather was hot and we had, that day, visited two caverns, Covalanas and La Haza, both of them not far from Ramales in the province of Santander. However, now it was getting cool and fresh. A slight breeze was blowing while the sun sank, glowing red, behind the peaks. We smoked, and as we smoked we looked right before us. The scents of the field came wafted toward us. We could feel the world was vast and wide. We could almost hear it breathe.

"I've never been in one of those caves," said the host. "What's so wonderful about them that you come here all the way from Germany to see them?"

"Haven't you ever heard of prehistoric pictures?" queried Alcalde del Rio.

"Yes, yes, of course, but I've never been able even to imagine what they can look like. What *do* they look like?"

"They look like what they are—paintings, regular paintings on the walls or roofs of caverns, paintings made by prehistoric men back in what's called the Ice Age."

"But how could they paint? Where did they get the colors from?"

"Well, there's ochre, that's found in the hills, and there's black manganese earth, there's iron oxide, perhaps chalks too. . . ."

"But what did they put the colors on with? What did they use as a medium?"

"Apparently animal fats," I put in, "but the question hasn't been very satisfactorily answered yet. Oil colors, for instance, on a damp stone surface, usually run, so there must have been something else added to the fats. Some specialists think that this something else may have been blood. If this was so then the binding agent would have been hematin. Others think that honey may have been employed, still others hold that the colors were just mixed with water and that they owe their marvelous state of preservation to the natural damp of the rock surfaces."

"And what's your own opinion?" he asked.

"To tell the truth I've really got no very strong or fixed opinion on the subject. I don't feel that I'm fitted to judge. A good deal of chemical research is necessary, maybe then the key to the mystery may be found, but the fact is that, up to now, we haven't discovered it."

"But hasn't anyone tried?"

"Surely. In Germany, for instance, there's a chemist who's gone so deeply into the problem that he's set up a special laboratory in his varnish factory. Possibly he may be lucky enough to discover the secret."

"Do you come across all sorts of colors in the paintings?" went on the innkeeper who, like many of his fellow countrymen, once their interest is aroused, was quite indefatigable in his questioning.

"No, there's no blue or green. For these no colored earths were available and there wasn't any stone which could be pounded up and powdered so as to give these pigments."

"By the way," asked Alcalde del Rio, "is green not found in the paintings of the so-called 'primitive' peoples?"

"Well, the Bushmen of South Africa used neither blue nor green. Of course, in other arts both blue and green were common enough. In China, for instance, much green was employed, though I think it's found only in historical times. The Chinese reduced emeralds to powder and so obtained a marvelous, durable pigment. In the pictures of the Sung dynasty, for instance, you are always coming across this entrancing, bright, brilliant emerald green."

"How do you think men of the Ice Age prepared their colors?" went on the innkeeper . . . "but don't answer directly; wait a minute or two. I've got to go and pour out a couple of glasses of *cerveza* and then I'll be back."

Under the last rays of the setting sun, the houses before us turned bright red and the tops of the trees shone all gilded. The colors of the landscape seemed deepened and enriched by some inner glow in the mild warmth of the dying day.

Two or three peasants walked past, then women and children came along. They were all laughing and chattering.

Our host was with us once more.

"You were going to tell me how the colors were prepared."

"Yes; well, that's something we can be quite certain about. Plenty of hollowed stones, that is to say mortars, have been found and in many of them there are still traces of color left. It was on and in such stones that the pigments were pounded until they were as fine as powder."

"We discovered stones like that at Altamira," said Alcalde del Rio, "and in one spot a whole stock of colors. On a little stone bench or slab lay crayons of all the colors they had in those days. They were neatly arranged side by side just as the men of the Ice Age had left them. Many of the crayons were sharpened so that they resembled the lipsticks ladies use nowadays. Of course, it's quite possible that in prehistoric times, also, people painted themselves and touched themselves up with color."

"Oh, that's not only possible, it's almost certain," I countered, "for all peoples at the same level of culture as that of late palaeolithic man, that's to say peoples who are hunters and food-gatherers and do not practice any sort of agriculture, paint themselves on the occasion of religious festivals, for ritual and cult reasons. Among such peoples are the South African Bushmen, the prairie Indians of North America, the Australian aborigines and the Vedda forest-dwellers of Ceylon. Of course, some agriculturalist peoples also paint themselves, but the practice is not so widespread or so general as it is among hunting communities. I should guess that painting of the body came before the making of pictures upon rock surfaces, and that possibly the former practice, in a measure, suggested the latter."

"What I find so astounding is how prehistoric men got the idea of making pictures upon walls and how they knew it was possible to paint on rocks and that the stone surface would hold the colors."

"Yes, I agree"—my words were directed to the innkeeper—"but we've got some evidence for the transition from painted bodies to painted rocks. For this, indeed, El Castillo is so important. It offers examples of the switchover . . . in that cave we've got a whole mass of paintings of hands and those hands must first of all have been covered with pigment and then pressed against the rock-face. At El Castillo such painted hands appear to be the most ancient of the pictures; at any rate, they underlie the archaic paintings of early Aurignacian date."

"True enough," put in Alcalde del Rio, "but the queerest thing is that many of the hands are 'negatives,' that is to say stencils, for they show the surface of the hand uncolored but surrounded with color. So it's evident that the hands must have been held outspread, pressed against the rock, while color was blown or powdered over them, so, as I say, the surface of the inside of the hand is uncolored while the pigment makes an aura or aureole around it. Obviously, men tried out all sorts of experiments. There are a good many representations of hands at Altamira too, and they are also unquestionably the oldest paintings there."

"And you've noticed, of course, that there are plenty of hand-stencils or impressions with a finger or the joint of a finger or fingers missing?"

"Sure enough. I've often noticed them at El Castillo, for instance, as well as at Altamira. What do you think these mutilations meant?"

"Oh, they're the sign of religious practices."

"Religious?" put in our host while his eager black eyes searched the faces of both Alcalde del Rio and myself. "Wait a minute or two, I've got to hear this, but I must go and look after my customers a bit."

By now the sun had disappeared behind the hills down whose slopes a most pleasant freshness was creeping into the valley while a delicate veil of mist spread slowly over the landscape. The mountains, high above the houses, had by now turned a deep blue. The sky, however, was suffused with a faint glow and had paled. Below, it was almost yellow and then it merged, by subtle gradations, upward into a luminous, almost transparent azure that shimmered around the sadness of distance. A scene magic in its fascination; the blue of the hills in exquisite harmony with hues of the heavens, hues so delicate as to be almost incredible. I was entranced. Such colors of surpassing beauty are altogether different from what I was accustomed to in my own country.

When the innkeeper got back to us he went on:

"You were going to talk about religion, the religion of prehistoric man, man of the Ice Age. . . ."

"Yes, I was, but you're sure that you'll not be bored?"

"No, no, I don't think so; anything to do with religion interests me, especially with origins, beginnings . . . and, as you can well imagine, I don't often get guests I can talk to about such matters."

"Good. Well, if you're sure you're not going to be bored and if it's quite understood that we're going to do nothing to disturb this divine evening, then I'd like to tell you what I think about the whole question. Let's see, to begin with, there's this problem of the mutilated hands, of hands with fingers and joints chopped off. Obviously this mutilation had some very definite significance and signification. It was a rite by which men dedicated themselves to some divine power. Similar practices survive among several of the so-called 'primitive' peoples of our day. To ensure that some venture will be accomplished successfully, they devote to a divinity a joint, for instance, of their fingers; that is to say, a part of their body is promised in sacrifice. If the venture is successful, then the hand is mutilated as agreed upon between the worshipper and his deity or spirit. The devotee offers up something which is, to him, very precious. That's how things still happen in some parts of our modern world and among peoples at more or less the same stage of social and economic evolution. There are so many examples to be found of this ritual mutilation that we are forced to conclude such practices throw a light upon what took place long ages ago; in prehistoric times, in fact."

"So you think that men of the Old Stone Age, of many thousands of years ago, had some sort of belief in a god?"

"That's certainly my opinion. When men offer up sacrifice, when they perform acts of solemn dedication, why, then it seems to me obvious that the sacrifice and the dedication must be made to some sort of divinity, to some spirit or supernatural power."

"Is it your feeling that these prehistoric men had many gods or only one?"

"Strange as it may seem, I think that we can today give a fairly definite answer to that question. It is true that up to a few years ago this whole subject was very shadowy and obscure; however, some notable discoveries have now shed a good deal of light upon the question. During the nineteenth century the belief was widely held that monotheism was obviously derived from polytheism, that's to say that a cult of many spirits or deities came before that of one deity. The latter part of the last century was so strongly influenced by the doctrine of physical evolution that the idea of gods was also thought of in terms of physical evolution. But then the revelation of prehistoric, of late palaeolithic, art did much to shatter the belief in a spiritual evolution parallel with the physical; so also, in a measure, was the case with religion.

"Ethnographical studies had gradually demonstrated that many peoples living in the most 'primitive' conditions, as hunters and food-gatherers, appeared to have a definite belief in a single, supreme deity. Investigations undertaken, for instance, among the Bushmen of South Africa, the Fuegians of Southern Patagonia, the Australian aborigines, and other peoples of a comparable way of life, tended to demonstrate the prevalence of such beliefs.

"In my opinion this evidence is valuable for enabling us to judge of the religious ideas of men of the last Ice Age and, indeed, of men who flourished before the last Ice Age; of men, that is, who lived in the warm period, the so-called Riss-Würm Interglacial, which lasted for many, many thousands of years before the onset of the last Ice Age." *

"But how's that possible? How can we know what peo-

* The author adopts a chronology that sets the Riss-Würm Interglacial at from 183,000 to 118,000 years ago. (*Translator's note.*)

ple believed an immensely long time ago, when there was no writing? People who left no traditions to come down to us? How can you discover what people thought, felt, and believed? How can you find those things out just by digging in caves?"

"Yes, I'll admit," I said in reply to our host's question, "I'll admit it does all seem fantastically mysterious and improbable, yet just listen to this: in the Swiss Alps there are caves that lie above the three-thousand-foot line, up in the mountains; there are two of them, they're called Wildemannlisloch and Drachensloch. And just because these caverns are situated relatively so high up, it's clear they could not have been utilized by men in Ice Age times, for during then the whole of the region where these caves are was covered over with a thick mantle of glaciers. Obviously, therefore, the caves must have been used and frequented by man before the onset of the last Ice Age glaciers, in other words our Wildemannlisloch and Drachensloch were homes—or sanctuaries—much earlier . . . in the warm period of the last, that is, the Riss-Würm, Interglacial.

"The discovery aroused a good deal of interest and attention, so a Swiss scientist, Bächler, began excavations in the caverns, where he turned up artifacts and stone implements of so-called 'Mousterian' type, such as were made and used by Neanderthaloid Man, who flourished, we know, before the onset of the last Ice Age (and, indeed, survived for a considerable time during that age). The Neanderthaloids were of a more rugged build than that of any 'modern' man now living upon this earth; they had retreating foreheads and their faces were rather 'snouty,' and though far from being 'ape-men,' they certainly differed a good deal in appearance from the creators of the Ice Age paintings, who were 'modern' men, more or less like ourselves. We are, in fact, very largely their descendants. These 'modern' men —artists and painters—are often referred to by the generic name of 'Cro-Magnon,' though the Cro-Magnon was but one of the human types to flourish in Western Europe in late palaeolithic times.

"These Neanderthaloids (who take their name from the Neanderthal site near Düsseldorf where the first of their bones were discovered) are, today, quite familiar to us, since more than thirty Neanderthaloid skeletons (or parts of skeletons) have been found.

"Now for the evidence about the Neanderthaloids' beliefs.

"In the caverns Bächler came across what may be called stone chests. In these, cave-bear skulls were piled up. There were skulls and also certain other bones, all arranged one beside the other. And this was not all, for a German, Hörmann, discovered the same sort of arrangement in the Petershöhle, a cavern near Velden in Central Franconia. It seems certain that these caves did not serve as larders, since, had this been the case, other portions of the cave-bear skeletons would have been preserved. It looks as though there could be only one explanation for this careful storing away of beasts' remains. They must be the relics of some sort of sacrifice. And sacrifice, at least as we understand the word, is something offered by man to a higher being, to some sort of divinity.

"In my opinion, therefore, the Neanderthaloid men held a belief in some sort of divinity, though, of course, excavations tell us nothing about the nature of this divinity. Nevertheless, much evidence has been preserved of what men thought, believed, and experienced. We can see that thoughts, beliefs, and traditions may survive from epoch to epoch. Some continued, for instance, into the Ice Age following the Interglacial, and then, as the ice gradually melted, and peoples moved up northward, following the retreating animals, some of these beliefs were preserved through the millennia, until the present day.

"For instance, what looks like the same sort of sacrifice —the same fashion of piling up bear-skulls that was performed by the remote Neanderthaloids—can still be found in Siberia among hunting peoples such as the Gilyaks and the Yakuts, or, again, among the Ainu, the aboriginal inhabitants of Japan who live on in the northern island of Hokkaido. The Ainu offer up bears' heads and carry out bear-sacrifice which reminds us very much of the Neanderthaloids' practices many millennia ago.

"And now for another proof, and this throws a good deal of light upon our problem, I think; Professor Zotz discovered prehistoric bear-skulls in Silesia, and from these certain teeth were missing. To this day among some tribes in Siberia, teeth are extracted from the bear's skull, and during the operation magic formulas are chanted and oaths taken.

"It looks as though among these Siberian tribes certain beliefs and conceptions have been preserved which go back to Ice Age times—and maybe before that. Among these Siberian tribes there is a rather general belief in a sole deity —rather than in a pantheon—a unique deity, creator of the earth, of life and of mankind, of the heavens and all that they contain. Therefore, in my opinion, anyway, it looks very much as though when the Neanderthaloids extracted teeth from bear-skulls offered up in sacrifice these most ancient men were honoring a single deity.

"Sacrificial practices are also evident at a site called Ahrensburg, in Holstein; the place dates from the end of the palaeolithic, of the last Ice Age. Rust, when excavating in a lake of glacial formation, came across a portion of a reindeer that was pierced. It was obvious that reindeer, with stones weighing down their bodies, were cast into the pool. Sacrifice again, an offering to some divinity. And here, at El Castillo, the mutilated hands are also signs of sacrifice and that's why I'm so anxious to see them . . . at some festival in honor of the spirits, men painted themselves and repaired to caverns where, in the bowels of the earth, reigned darkness, the unknown and the mysterious. And their painted hands they pushed against the rock wall; they saw that the color stayed, that its traces did not vanish . . . so, too, the spirits can see and they command man to mutilation, to sacrifice."

"In fact," put in Alcalde del Rio, "these caverns were more or less like our churches today. . . ."

"Yes, indeed, that's very true; the deities were for man in those days just as unknown, as far off—and as near—as incomprehensible, and as unexplainable as they are for us today. We have thought about the idea of God for centuries, for millennia even, but I don't think we're much nearer a solution of the problem now than we ever were."

"But do you think that prehistoric man's concept of God was anything like that held today?"

"Ah, that's what I wouldn't dare to say. It looks to me as though there was an early belief in a deity as the creator of all things and that this concept was followed by another in which the idea of deity is spread out among several distinct divinities, and that this latter idea is then followed by yet another belief in a single deity . . . so I don't think that present-day monotheism can be compared with that of the Ice Age.

"The Ice Age is, too, a period when mankind was younger, when the human spirit was awakening to many things. We can imagine a time when astonishment was still aroused by man's surroundings . . . just as some father and mother of a race are held to have created everything the tribe possesses, so then must there be a father-creator, an originator who has made everything that lies around man, who has supplied the earth, the beasts, the heavens. The world looks obvious, as yet there is no problem of good or evil . . . no god of vengeance or retribution, no problem of grace, no feeling of guilt or sin . . . or any of those things to which men in later days have devoted so much thought and time.

"All that sort of thing must come much later when habits of thought and language become more developed, mature, and complicated. I am inclined to hold that the multiplicity of deities derives from the many visages of divinity . . . it stems from evil, revenge, temptation, sense of guilt . . . it arises from war and tempest, from the rain and the vision of the heavenly bodies. Of course, in a more advanced way of thought, unity is recognized in multiplicity, the incomprehensible that informs all experience. . . .

"And so, we have again the concept of a single deity that is creator and all-father, because, of course, above and beyond us there lies forever the great realm of things unknown and unknowable, incomprehensible and everlasting. There's a poem of Goethe's—*Procemion*—that's rather appropriate to such thoughts.

[The celebrated verses of Goethe's *Procemion* might be translated:

> In name of him who did himself create
>   Eternally eternity creating,
> In his name who commandeth Trust and Faith
>   Confidence, Activity and Puissance,
> In that great name which though so often named
>   By its own essence must unknown remain.
>
> So far the ear, so far the eye may range,
>   Familiar only findest thou like him,
> And thy spirit's highest flight of flame is
>   Satisfied by image and by likeness.
> It lures thee on, it draws thee blithely up
>   And, when thou wanderest, decks each place and way,
> Thou countest not nor reckonest any time
>   For every step is incommensurable.
>
>   —*Translator*]

"So, it seems to me, we have to be content with likeness and image . . . the risen god, the dying god and the dead . . . image of the waxing and waning of the moon, and of life and of all that exists. Then again, there's the highest form of sacrifice, in which the god offers himself for mankind instead of mankind sacrificing itself to the god . . . the sacrifice of Wotan, of Quetzalcoatl in ancient Mexico, of Purusha in India. And maybe it's just the very beginning of this sacrifice-idea that we can behold here at El Castillo. . . ."

I felt that I had held forth long enough, too long, perhaps, so I came to a full stop.

It was now quite dark. The stars had pierced the heavens and soon the moon's radiance would bathe the whole scene. It was very still. Lights from many windows gleamed into the dying twilight.

Our host it was who broke the stillness.

"Tomorrow I'll come with you to the cavern, if you'll allow me. But I'd rather no one in the village saw me. Demons lurk in the caverns, you know, evil spirits! . . . The people here about might think I'd made a pact with the Devil if they know I've gone off exploring caves. . . ."

The morning was fresh, dewy and brilliantly clear. The sun was already high up in the heavens when the four of us, Rita, Alcalde del Rio, the innkeeper, and myself, left the house. The road leads out from the village and crosses a big, humpbacked bridge that straddles the Rio Paz and thence winds up into the hills and the heights. They were all almost bare, and the landscape was made up of stones and rocks, weeds and low brushwood. The way was not very long and soon we were at the entrance to the grotto.

"You'll notice how big the entrance is," remarked Alcalde del Rio; "when I discovered the cave in 1903, the way in was so low and so well hidden that again and again, on later occasions, I missed it altogether when I wanted to revisit the cavern.

"Right at the entrance is an encampment-site of Ice Age Man. Obermaier conducted extensive excavations here and from them it is certain that El Castillo was not only frequented by late palaeolithic 'modern' men, but also by Neanderthaloids. For, underlying the rich deposits laid down by the men who painted the pictures—men of Aurignacian, Solutrean, and Magdalenian cultures—comes the Neanderthaloid stratum, that is to say the one containing Mousterian artifacts, stone implements and tools. I was often present while Obermaier was digging and the results he obtained were very impressive. Above, in the Ice Age strata, were found the remains of 'cold' fauna—such beasts as reindeer, musk-oxen and mammoths—while, lower down, the fauna was of quite a different sort, especially when we came to deposits of the last Interglacial; that is, layers containing Mousterian artifacts. Here, instead of reindeer, was stag; instead of mammoth, elephant (i.e. *elephas antiquus*); and in place of the woolly rhinoceros, Merck's rhinoceros. Yes, and now just think of this, if you please . . . the lowest level of all, here at El Castillo, belongs to the last Ice Age but one, that is to say to the Riss glaciation, and in this stratum were found artifacts of Acheulian type associated with cave bears' remains and with those of reindeer once more. This lowest, deepest, and last El Castillo stratum dates back to many, many tens of thousands of years ago.*

"In fact, this entrance-site was just like a chronicle of the earth's history, or, at least, of man's story. We turned over this chronicle, page by page, reaching ever farther and farther back into the past. On the top, in the uppermost layers, we were in the time of the paintings, in the Age of Art: below came the warm Interglacial period, and then, still farther down, full Ice Age conditions once again. As you once remarked, Herr Kühn, nowhere else are such clear and definite monuments and chronicles of the far-distant past found in such beautifully arranged contexts. Almost all the other caverns I know of, or have explored, contain three, or at the most four, strata. In no other site are there so many, one below the other, as at El Castillo."

"Oh, there's no doubt about it, El Castillo's absolutely unique," I put in. "We're delighted to have an opportunity of seeing it at last . . . you get quite a different impression when you've been to a place and not just read about it. By the way, did you discover any small art-objects in the deposits at El Castillo?"

"Not very many. In the upper Magdalenian strata there was a staff with a hole punched in it, one of the so-called

---

* According to the chronology the author has adopted, the Riss glaciation lasted from about 236,000 to 183,000 years ago. (*Translator's note.*)

bâtons de commandement, you know. It was adorned with the engraving of a stag which, at one time, had been filled in with ochre. In a lower Magdalenian layer we came across several shoulder-blades engraved with heads of hinds. There were also, just as at Altamira, some sketch-blocks

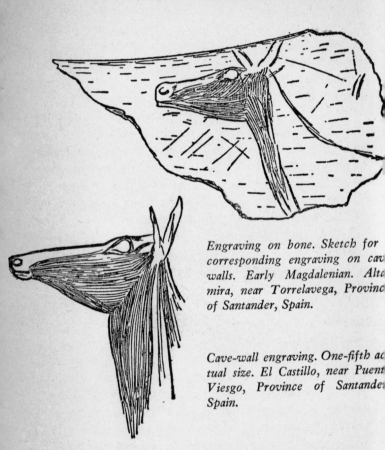

Engraving on bone. Sketch for corresponding engraving on cave walls. Early Magdalenian. Altamira, near Torrelavega, Province of Santander, Spain.

Cave-wall engraving. One-fifth actual size. El Castillo, near Puente Viesgo, Province of Santander, Spain.

from which—in some cases, anyway—large paintings upon the cave's walls can be dated, since the latter pictures were enlarged from the small sketches or, if you like, the sketches served as models for the big frescoes. But, generally speaking, what we got in the way of art-objects was not very noteworthy, and, if you compare what we found here with the splendid discoveries of small works of art at a site such as La Laugerie Basse in France, the booty we came upon here was insignificant."

"Maybe there were schools which specialized in one branch of artistic creation or another. To take one example, there are no wall-paintings at La Laugerie Basse. By the way, how many have you identified here at El Castillo?"

"There are, altogether, a hundred and thirty-three pictures in this cave. They begin quite near the entrance and are scattered about, without any apparent plan or design, over the whole cavern right to the farthest end."

"Was there any habitation site found farther inside the cave or was there only the one at the entrance?"

"No, only the one at the entrance. Farther inside this cavern, as, indeed, inside all the others, men never lived. Only the entrances were used as dwellings. The farthest recesses were used for religious ends and the passages and galleries leading to these sanctuaries were, of course, often decorated with paintings and engravings."

Thereupon we entered the grotto. The entrance hall is wide and spacious. As the floor rises rather sharply, we slipped and slithered about a good deal in the mud and damp clay. This entrance hall is, of course, entirely without engravings, drawings, or paintings, a usual state of things in all prehistoric caverns. Through two narrow passages the way leads in to an enormous chamber. We groped our way along by the right-hand side wall. Then, soon, another gallery opened before us. Alcalde del Rio raised his lamp. We were surrounded by Hands. I placed my own hand on one of the paintings. The two outlines coincided. These were the imprints of the hands of men and most of them were stencils—negatives—and therefore surrounded by a blur of pigment which had been blown onto the wall. The number of left hands is very striking. I counted only nine right hands but no less than thirty-five left hands. It looks, therefore, as though even in those remote days men were mostly right-handed. The left hand would be free when color was held in the right; so it was the left hand that was laid upon the surface of the rocky wall. For the rest, these imprints of hands are almost exactly like those of men of today. The fingers and palms are strong-looking and rather large. Only a few of the stencils appear to have been made by younger men or boys and probably none at all by women.

At El Castillo there are imprints of hands underlying pictures of elephants; these drawings consist only of outlines and are, indeed, markedly archaic. We can assign them to an early Aurignacian period. The hands, however, are obviously older than the elephant pictures and are, therefore, probably among the most ancient examples of painting which exist in this world. On this same portion of the rock walls there is a third layer of paintings whose pictures consist of polychrome representations of hinds, together with some very large and strikingly lifelike paintings of bisons. These figures belong to the peak-period of late palaeolithic art, that is to say to the mid-Magdalenian.

The many red blobs and dots are puzzling. It is difficult to find any meaning for them. Here, for instance, are seventeen of them all in a row. Here again, six, and there, seven. Here is a stalagmite marked with eleven dots in a row and on one line. It is tempting to try to guess at the significance of these things. Were they indications of direction with a note of the number of steps to be taken? We started from the places with dots and took the number of steps indicated. Often, indeed, we did land up against pictures, but more often our calculations did not lead us anywhere. It is possible that the relevant pictures have disappeared. But it is also possible, if not probable, that the dots and blobs had some quite other meaning. Maybe the number of heads of game. Who knows?

We soon found the heavy murk of the cavern to be oppressive and, in fact, rather sinister. Water trickled down and oozed under our feet. Great blocks of stone often barred the way. The ground got even more slippery. We stumbled on, our lamps swaying and swinging. We righted ourselves again and then our lights flashed against walls, and more walls . . . here pictures of wild horses, ibex, gazelles, bison. And then, here, the rents torn by the cave bears' murderous claws. These scratches and strokes, it seems most probable, suggested the idea of engraving to early man, prompted him to draw in the clay of the caverns with his fingers and then, later, with flint or other stone instruments on the rock surfaces.

We were in a very narrow passage that led on apparently without end—and in fact it does extend more than three hundred and fifty yards into the bowels of the mountain. Almost at the end of this passage we found the finest of all the El Castillo pictures. It is that wonderful portrait of an elephant that has been so often reproduced.

Then we turned around, fumbled about, stooped, clambered over the rocks, extricated ourselves and, finally, once more could stand upright. We took a different way back. The cavern, indeed, is full of branching galleries and side-passages, and if one were not with someone who knows them, it would be impossible to find one's way about—or out again. The ground sank sharply and then rose again and once more dropped down. At one spot there is a whole mass of drawings—a giant stag, a *cervus elaphus*, with hinds and ibex. The heads of these hinds are very like those of sketches discovered in one of the undisturbed strata. Then there are also sketches of bison, with clever shading effects and executed in a style quite different from that of the paintings. There are also several wild horses, one upon the other.

More of the enigmatic signs. Some might be meant for huts, others for hedges or fencing. Still others are shield-shaped.

"What do you think these signs could have meant?" asked Alcalde del Rio.

"I can't say; still, somehow, I don't think they are supposed to be huts, all the same. I should rather say traps and snares for wild beasts. Hunting peoples today still employ very strong gins or traps. They are constructed of long stakes and pieces of wood. The beasts are driven toward and into these things, and when the animal bumps up against the pieces of wood, these fall together and hold the creature fast, when it is fairly easy to kill."

"You may be right . . . traps . . . I hadn't thought of that; neither had Breuil, I think. . . ."

"Of course, I don't know if my guess is the right one, but I can't find any other explanation for these strange signs."

When we got out into the open again it was noon. We sought out a shady bush and settled down beside it. The host of the inn uncorked the bottles and served out cold chicken. We ate with good appetite, but even as we ate we felt, I think, that around us was the atmosphere of past millennia.

"Now we must make for another cavern that lies in this same range. It's called La Pasiega and there's a book that's been written about it," announced Alcalde del Rio.

"When was La Pasiega discovered?"

"Oh, much later than El Castillo. I found that in 1903 and it was not until the spring of 1911 that Obermaier conducted his excavations at El Castillo, but while he was at work all the caves of the region were searched for paintings. The countryside is rich enough in grottoes, but, naturally enough, very few of them are prehistoric. However, one day a laborer came and announced to us that he'd discovered an entirely new cave. It was at once explored and proved to be adorned with many pictures. I myself happened to be at El Castillo at that time and I took an active part in the search and found a number of painted passages.

"There's one very great peculiarity about La Pasiega. The passages are on different levels, they are over and under one another, so that if we had not followed Ariadne's example and taken a ball of thread with us, we should never have been able to find the way out again. Now we've put up little signposts against the walls of the grotto.

They're a great help, it's true; still, it's very far from easy to find one's way and it's still necessary to take some thread or string with us.

"And, first of all, it's very difficult to discover the cave itself, for the entrance is a hole in the earth; you go down a sheer drop . . . and the hole is screened with bush. I only hope I'll be able to identify it again. The cave must lie right up there. . . ."

So we started off on our hunt for the entrance to La Pasiega, but, to begin with, there was no pathway at all. The ground looked quite untrodden, as though the cavern had not been visited again since Obermaier's season of excavations. Obviously it was no one's business to worry about a path to an isolated grotto. We made our way, rather painfully, through low-growing but thick-set brushwood that ripped our clothes, stabbed us through our stockings and socks and pierced through the soles of our shoes.

"I know it's somewhere here, just near here, I'm sure of it."

But neither Alcalde del Rio nor any others of us could discover where the hole was. We hunted for it above and we hunted for it below; one of us scrambled away to the left and another to the right, but no sign of any hole in the ground. An hour—a long hour—went by, and we were still searching.

"All this scrub and bush has changed a lot through the years. I must confess I can't find the cave, and I think we'd better give up and turn back home. . . ."

Just then Rita's voice came echoing down the hill. She had lit upon a hole that seemed to drop down deep into the earth. Maybe it was the cave?

It was. We were, needless to say, overjoyed. The hole was quite hidden by a bush and was almost impossible to find. The aperture opened, as Alcalde del Rio had said, directly into the earth, and moreover, the opening was so small that a man could only with difficulty slip down

Ground plan of La Pasiega Cavern, near Puente Viesgo, Province of Santander, Spain: (1) Existing entrance. (2) Main concentration of paintings. (3) Isolated pictures.

through it. With great care, and very gingerly, Alcalde del Rio made his way down first. He soon disappeared and was followed by Rita and then the innkeeper and then by me. Down at the bottom of the drop is a very narrow entrance-way, and first of all we had to crouch in a constricted passage that dropped steeply downward, where one had to be very careful about one's movements. Suddenly, we were confronted by a veritable labyrinth or maze of passages. Corridors led off on every side; they passed under and above one another, they met and then they diverged. We kept close together, in Indian file, and so as to run no risk of getting lost we were never out of calling distance one from another. Alcalde del Rio took a ball of thread from his pocket, fastened one end of the string securely to a stone and then, holding the skein tight in his hand, he set off with us trailing behind him.

"Look, here are the arrows and signposts we put up, but they're not enough. Much safer to take a ball of thread."

The cavern broadened out. Soon we could walk quite upright. On every side were pictures. Many were engravings, but most were paintings in red, yellow, or black.

"Do you happen to know how many pictures there are in this whole cave?" I asked.

"Oh, yes, we counted them often enough. There are two hundred and twenty-six paintings and thirty-six engravings, that's to say, two hundred and sixty-two pictures in all. Most of them, as you'll notice, are of Aurignacian date, but some belong to the early Magdalenian phases. The finest and most significant period of all, the mid-Magdalenian, is not represented at La Pasiega.

"Just look at this," he went on. "Obermaier found at El Castillo the sketch-block that served as the model for this painting. The sketch was lying in a stratum of lower Magdalenian date. This wall-painting here at La Pasiega is therefore datable, at least approximately. Notice these many successive layers; the style of the datable picture turns up again and again."

"Surely, and I'd say one can trace the same hand, that it was one and the same artist who executed the pictures," I said.

"And here"—he pointed—"under this group there lie other Aurignacian pictures. You can recognize their much simpler, smoother style. In Aurignacian times, drawings and paintings represented outlines only. Shading is very rare, and when it does occur it is only in what might be called an elementary or primitive form."

"What I'd like to know is why prehistoric men painted over already existing pictures and painted over them again and again," said the innkeeper.

"I'd say there were two reasons for that," I answered him. "First of all, there was the need to economize pigments which were certainly most valuable and rare. In this picture, for instance, we've apparently got a case in point."

And I indicated a picture of horses where it was quite clear that underlying traces of color belonging to older paintings had been utilized for the picture of the top layer.

"The second reason, and I'm inclined to think that it is the more important one, is that the pictures were held to bring good luck in the chase, and therefore the wizard used what had been proved to be efficacious; he utilized the same emplacement, the same picture, many times. In this manner, the representation itself got changed in the shuffle, so to speak. Bisons were made out of mammoths, as we can see for ourselves at Font-de-Gaume, for instance, and in several other grottoes."

Then we caught sight of a wonderful horse standing out large and proud; a tarpan, a kind of wild horse with upright, thick-set mane . . . and the ibexes, the aurochs, the bisons, stags, and hinds . . . there is also an elephant—but it is unique—at La Pasiega. And there are no reindeer at all.

Scattered about on the walls are to be seen "fences" and other mysterious signs. El Castillo is rich enough in them, but La Pasiega has many more. Here is an animal with a "snare" painted on its neck; maybe through this sign the animal was magically controlled. Of course we cannot even guess what every sign was intended to represent, but it does seem probable that many of them are traps, enclosures, palings, lattices, pitfalls, snares. . . .

At La Pasiega the old original entrance to the cave can be seen. Such approaches are rare, for in most of the prehistoric caves they have collapsed and are no longer accessible. Of course this ancient entrance is quite devoid of pictures, though the walls do bear some mysterious signs. One is inclined to call them a sort of primitive script with representations of hands. The present entrance to La Pasiega was undoubtedly formed in comparatively recent times and by the combined action of wind, weather, and rainwater.

"These signs, these hands, must signify the taking possession of the cavern, I think," suggested Alcalde del Rio.

"That's very possible, but we can't say for sure . . . the meaning of such signs, I'm afraid, is likely to remain unknown to us forever."

"Anyway, it's my opinion that the two hands together were a sign of possession."

"That may well be true in many instances, for signs of hands to indicate possession do occur in many cultures we know of. So, when one comes to think of it, that may well be the case here. You've probably hit upon the right solution."

As we left La Pasiega, twilight was already dropping over the summits and heights. When we had wriggled out of that hole in the ground, and jerked ourselves upward by shoving out our arms and knees together at the same time, we felt very tired and exhausted indeed. For a few minutes we rested by the insignificant entrance leading to so many marvels, and then we made our way down into the valley.

Wall paintings in red: One-twentieth actual size. La Pasiega Cave, near Puente Viesgo, Province of Santander, Spain.

That evening we sat once more upon the bench in front of the inn—Rita, Alcalde del Rio, the innkeeper, and myself. The sun had already sunk. It was later than when we had taken our places on the preceding day. The first stars had begun to shine. The sky was very dark and yet clear, a sort of transparent darkness. Only slowly did the moon's radiance grow bright upon the village dwellings.

"I'd never have thought a cave could be so fascinating," opined our host. "I'd never have believed so much could have been preserved from such ancient times and, also, I'd never have imagined we could find out so much about the religion of prehistoric times. You know, we Spaniards are very religious and this sort of thing moves us more than, apparently, it moves you."

"Yes, our modern world in the West has practically lost religion altogether. If one has traveled in other parts of the globe, say, for instance, in India, one soon realizes how much religion means to the Indians. It is, indeed, what provides the content, the sense, the value of life for them. For us, I think, religion is something like art, or poetry, like the theatre or music; in fact, just a means of escape from the daily round. There are only a very few people who are really possessed by religion. Religion remains on the edge of our lives. We think about it, if at all, only on the occasion of great festivals, Easter or Christmas, or we are reminded of religion by ceremonies, such as baptisms, weddings, burials. So it comes about that it is very difficult for us to understand and to appreciate other cultures in which religion plays a primordial role, the cultures, say, of India or of Tibet, or maybe of our Western Europe in the last Ice Age. We can hardly imagine a life wholly subjected to religious considerations, totally bound by sacred laws; in fact, it is only with the greatest difficulty that we manage to reconstruct some sort of picture of the Middle Ages in our own Europe, a time when religion was not only a living thing but when men felt that they could realize themselves to the full only in God and in following his commandments."

We sat quite still and smoked. The heaven was full of stars, the moon by this time brilliantly shining and its light falling white and ghostly upon the streets, about the houses, and on the mountains that closed our horizon.

We had seen much that day. We had looked back into the early thoughts of man. We had gazed into the origins of art and into the beginnings of religion upon this earth of ours.

For the wizard, for the shaman, for the magician, the beast he painted must have been both parable and symbol,

and it is in and by similes, parables, that in all ages and
among all peoples religions live and thrive. After all, we
are no farther forward than was the man of the Ice Age;
what was mystery for him is also mystery for us—life,
birth, and death.

V: Tuc d'Audoubert

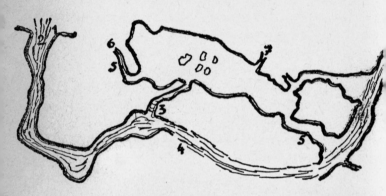

Ground plan of the Tuc d'Audoubert Cave, near Montesquieu-Avantès, Ariège Department, France: (1) Entrance. (2) The River Volp which flows through the mountain. (3) Steep ascent. (4) Unexplored ascent. (5) Signs. (6) Unexplored gallery. (7) The "Cat's Hole" ascent.

The sun was sinking crimson behind the peaks. The huge chain of the Pyrenees stood out as though drenched in blood. The motor was humming some sort of tune, always on the same note, and I was at the steering-wheel. The rhythmical noise, the effort of watching the road, absorbed my whole attention, and the highway twisted first to one bend and then to another while leading ever higher and higher up. It was getting quite cold. On the back seat, Rita and my old friend Count Bégouen, from Toulouse, had muffled themselves up in all the available rugs.

We were on our way back from the Barcelona Congress.
The year was 1926.

Soon, the countryside became quite bare. The stony soil
showed fewer and fewer patches of sparse and straggling
grass. To our right lay the Principality of Andorra which,
with San Marino, Liechtenstein, and Monaco, is one of the
small European states which have survived from the Middle
Ages. The road got steeper and steeper, the air colder and
colder, but before long we had crossed the divide and were
dropping down to Bourg-Madame on the frontier, the first
French village. In those days the customs people did not
hold one up for long, and very soon we had taken up our
quarters in a charming, friendly little hotel. After dinner,
as we were sitting over a bottle of the delicious local wine,
I thought the moment propitious for asking Bégouen's permission to visit the Tuc d'Audoubert. For he was not only
Professor of Prehistory at the University of Toulouse, but
the discoverer of the cave and, indeed, the owner of it and
of the surrounding property near Montesquieu-Avantès in
the Ariège department.

I approached the subject in a rather roundabout fashion,
but Bégouen at once saw what I was after and headed me
off.

"I'm much too old for caves, and the passage through
what we call the 'cat's hole'—that is, the connecting corridor between the main chambers—is so difficult to negotiate
that it would be quite hopeless for me to try to push
through. The fact is, I'll tell you quite frankly, I've got too
fat. Even right at the beginning, when my sons discovered
this passage, it was torture for me to wriggle through, and
that was in 1912 when I was much younger . . . but the
going was very hard indeed. I've often endeavored to
squeeze myself through more recently. I've pulled in my
belly—and, after all, it's not so very large. I had a good try,
but it was no good at all; moreover, the sides, the edges of
the aperture are far from smooth. My sons, in order to get
through, had to hack away at the stalagmites, for in the

course of ages the deposits of calcite had quite blocked up this 'cat's hole.' Just think of it; only one drop at a time, often only one drop a day, but each drop contains a tiny particle of calcium carbonate which remains . . . and this goes on for centuries, for millennia. First of all we get a little mound, then, later on, a pendentive, a hanging 'icicle,' and below it a sort of obelisk or pyramid, like a sugar-loaf. And it's all as hard as rock. The 'cat's hole,' as I've just told you, was blocked up and it was by mere chance that we managed to find any traces of an aperture at all.

"One of my sons was looking for prehistoric pictures and flashing his light against the walls when he noticed, all at once, that one part of the walls was covered with a mass of stalagmitic matter, but also appeared translucent. Obviously, beyond this wall of calcite there was another hall or chamber of some sort. So the boys set to work with their axes, cut through the stalagmites, and thus were able to penetrate into a part of the cavern that had been closed to all mortal eyes for thousands of years—since the end of the Ice Age, in fact.

"When they got back to the house that evening they were very excited indeed, and the next day I of course had to go with them to the cavern. And then it was that I found out I couldn't get through the 'cat's hole.' One of the boys pulled and another one shoved, but I was stuck fast in the middle with the spikes of stalagmite scratching and pricking my skin. Can you imagine, my dear Kühn, what it's like to have your skin rubbed off at every movement and yet be unable to either go on or go back? It's not very pleasant. My shirt was hanging in rags about my body. Then the lads started up again and, finally, after much sweating and pushing, they did get me through—naked. My trousers were left hanging on the spikes and my shirt had disappeared. The youngsters, of course, burst out laughing, but I didn't find it at all funny.

"However, your case is different, you're still slim enough and you'd be able to get through all right, but you mustn't count on me to act as a guide. It's a pity, for I'd have liked to go with you into the cave and discuss with you, on the spot, problems and questions we both take so much interest in. And now, I don't even know if my son Louis can go with you. He's very busy just at present, and you've got to allow a whole day for the visit. But I'll certainly talk to him about it and I sincerely hope that he'll be able to fix things up. You know, of course, that only very few people have seen the cave? Besides the boys and myself, only twelve persons. I can tell you who they were: old Cartailhac and Breuil, of course, Burkitt from Cambridge, MacCurdy from Yale, Birkner from Munich . . ."—here he added a few more names well known in scientific circles— "and we don't like people in the cave. For one thing, the going's much too difficult, and then, however much care is taken, there's always something changed, or knocked about or destroyed. Just think of it: a cave that's been visited by no human being since late palaeolithic times. On either side of you are skeletons of snakes and cave bears; then there are the imprints of prehistoric man's footsteps, Magdalenian footprints, preserved for more than ten thousand years. What a tragedy it would be if anyone should mutilate such things! So that's why we keep the caves well shut up. If my son takes you through them, then Rita and you will be the thirteenth and the fourteenth persons respectively to see the Tuc d'Audoubert. Everyone else merely repeats what he's picked up from our descriptions. Maybe, later on, people will be quoting yours, too."

I had, by this time, visited many prehistoric caves and I had never imagined that the Tuc d'Audoubert presented such difficulties; neither, I must confess, had I realized the caverns were so strictly closed and protected. And then there was another problem: how about Louis, would he be slender enough to squeeze through nowadays?

"When did Louis visit the Tuc d'Audoubert last?"

"Oh, about six months ago, I should say, more or less."

"And has he put on much weight lately?"

"Yes, perhaps he has, just a little, but I imagine he'd still be able to squeeze through the 'cat's hole.'"

"Has he . . . er . . . has he got much of a paunch?"

"Oh, yes, why that, of course," said Bégouen, laughing, while he made a semicircular gesture with his hands.

Then one of the natives of Bourg-Madame sat down beside us and began telling us what a hard winter they had had, with much snow on the mountains, and now a wretched harvest. We went to bed early, for the next day we would have a long run in front of us. During the night I dreamed that Louis had grown so fat he could not get through the hole at all but remained all day long hoisted up on the jagged stumps of stalagmites.

In the morning we headed straight for the Château de Pujol, which formerly belonged to the elder Bégouen but which he had, by this time, made over to his son Louis. When we got to Pujol and saw Louis we were much relieved. He was quite slim, even thin. I told him of my dream and he laughingly said:

"Of course I'll come with you tomorrow to the Tuc d'Audoubert, but we'll have to be off very early and we shan't get back till nightfall."

So that is how my dreams came true about the Tuc d'Audoubert.

Until the twilight fell about us we sat on the terrace of the château—the young couple, Count Bégouen and our two selves. We talked about everything under the sun, of travel, of Barcelona, and of the bygone Christmases the old Count used to spend with us at Cologne. He would arrive on Christmas Eve, help to decorate the Christmas tree, and then sing Christmas carols with us.

Before us stretched the long range of the Pyrenees. Below, meadows and woods, then, rising above them, the high mountains already decked with snow. As we gazed into the distance our thoughts took wings. We spoke of past ages and of the men who had here lived and loved and died in the time of the great glaciers. We could make out the hill

with the Tuc d'Audoubert, the hill on whose farther side
was the entrance to the then newly discovered cave called
Les Trois-Frères, because it was found by Count Bégouen's
three sons. It is clear that, in former times, the two caves
communicated, but the connecting passage had not been
discovered.

The next morning was cool and clear, the foliage all
sprinkled with autumnal dew. After breakfast on the terrace we put on our "speleological" clothes, each one took
a lamp, and we set off, the three of us, Rita, Louis Bégouen,
and I. After about half an hour's walk we got to a brook
called the Volp, swift-flowing, gurgling, its bed strewn
with boulders. The rays of the morning sun speckled from
the wavelets.

Louis announced that we had got to the cave's entrance,
but we could see no path, no aperture, nothing but a stream
which disappeared into a hillside . . . a stream very rapid
and impetuous.

"Now we'll get into the boat. You'll have to lie quite flat
on the bottom, for the water almost touches the ceiling. As
a matter of fact, in winter and in the spring, the brook's so
swollen that the cave gets water-logged and then there's
no question of exploring the Tuc d'Audoubert, which, by
the way, is quite often inaccessible even in the summer.
The best time of year is now—autumn."

We got in and lay down on the planking. Louis seized a
short oar and gave a good shove off; the boat shot along
and then bumped through the aperture. At first there was a
sort of twilight but it was soon completely dark. The rock-
vaulting bore right down upon us and in places scraped
the tops of the boat's sides. We slithered along round turn-
ings and still more corners. None of us said a word. It was
sinister and rather terrifying. But, eventually, the channel
widened out and we could discern a strip of beach. The
skiff stopped. We got out and straightened ourselves up on
the shore. A few yards farther on the Volp pours down
through a dark pit that it completely fills. Almost opposite

the spot where the subterranean river runs into the bowels of the earth, a narrow passage leads off through the rock-face.

We had dumped our luncheon-basket and the three lamps on the ground and squatted on stones until our eyes became accustomed to the gloom. Suddenly, there they were.

Pictures. Beasts engraved in the stones: bisons, reindeer, horses. Animal figures drawn with astonishing mastery of line and executed with firm, sure strokes. Right before us loomed a bison's head. One line defined the muzzle while, above, came the ears and the great horns. There are shamans here too, men wearing beast-masks, uncanny figures and weird. Another bison is struck by many arrows; a magic picture, as indeed were all those about us. From the head of a horse project P-shaped signs—these are not uncommon in prehistoric caverns. These objects appear to be boomerangs, projectiles slightly curved and, in the middle, thickened. Another magic picture.

Then we entered a spacious chamber. It was a fairy palace, an enchanted mansion, white and radiant. From the ceiling hung down stalactites while stalagmites rose up straight from the ground. This blazing assemblage so dazzles one's eyes that it is a good time before one can really see anything clearly, especially as in the middle of the cave there is a little lake, or a pond, that reflects every beam of light.

From time to time we could hear a drop fall onto the water's surface and in the uncanny stillness this ghostly drip, drip was most eerie.

Quite at the end of the hall is a sort of pillar or almost perpendicular chimney. The Bégouens cut steps into this and up it you have to clamber more than thirty feet of very steep climb. At the top is the opening to yet another gallery which leads to a small chamber out of which is a further passage. Here also are a few pictures: bisons and horses.

Then we got to the "cat's hole." First we could crouch

along, but then as the way got narrower we had to slither forward flat upon our faces. The passage is, as Bégouen said, exceedingly strait and narrow and low. We had to make ourselves as slim as possible, to press our arms close to our bodies and to wriggle forward snake-wise. But we did get through and could breathe again.

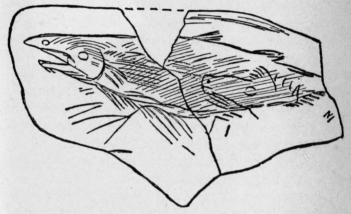

Engraving of a fish on stone: Mid-Magdalenian. Actual size. Trois-Frères Cavern, near Montesquieu-Avantès, Ariège Department, France.

More long passages, and then halls, further galleries and corridors and then something indescribably beautiful. An apartment like some enchanted festival-hall, some strange Gothic cathedral fashioned out of alabaster—a forest of stalagmites, a fairy-tale palace glittering, shimmering all white and pale yellows. Count Bégouen gave this chamber the name of Salle Cartailhac in honor of his famous predecessor in the chair of Prehistory at the University of Toulouse.

We made our way slowly through the great white room. By our lamps' light the stalagmites glowed ghostly, they threw shadows great and long. Then they flashed up again in blinding coruscations. Some of the icicles are quite thin and slim. If you strike them they ring out clear, bell-like notes, whereas other stalagmites yield much deeper tones.

Over in a corner, behind a mass of stalagmites, are traces of human footsteps impressed in the clay. The footprints of naked feet, the feet of prehistoric men. The "cat's hole" was forced only a short time ago. For millennia, with the exception of a few scientists and specialists, prehistorians and archaeologists, no one had stood in this cave but ourselves, no one for thousands of years. The footprints of Ice Age Man. You can notice how stalagmitic matter overlies the marks. During the millennia the footprints have become coated with calcite, therefore there can be no doubt about it, these imprints really do date back to upper palaeolithic times. As the ground has hardened, one can, strangely enough, take hold of these footprints and even push them up from beneath. If one examines the imprints closely one can recognize the marks of the wrinkles in the skin.

It is a queer, and an impressive, experience to hold in one's hand the cast of an Ice Age man's foot. We put the thing back again, with the greatest care. In this corner, too, a cave bear had its lair, for the impressions of its coat, of its muzzle, and of its feet are preserved in what was once soft clay. We got the feeling that a live cave bear was not far off and might, at any minute, loom up before us. For a moment we wondered if men and cave bears could have occupied the caverns at one and the same time; but no, of course that was impossible. Nowhere, indeed, are there intermingled traces. Everywhere, when they occur together, the footprints of the men are above those of the bears. Men came for the first time when the giant cave bears no longer had their lairs here.

A skeleton of a snake, coiled and twisted on the ground. No one has ever disturbed it. Cave bears' bones. A lower jaw, a good deal smashed about by human agency . . . other bones, all hacked about, scattered, cut up . . . and here, again, heaped as though to form a sort of barrier— against small animals maybe. The bear must have been

dead when men entered the cavern, though, of course, in
these remote recesses men did not make their homes. There
are nowhere here traces of charcoal, of hearths, there is no
refuse, there is no instrument, utensil, or tool used in daily
life. Men came hither, when they did come, for quite other
ends than even hunting, for the cave bears had left before
man arrived and, in any case, tracking these gigantic and
ferocious animals into their lairs would have been foolhardy
in the extreme. No, what attracted man into these grottoes
was their darkness, their mysterious and unknown quality;
in fact, here prehistoric man found himself in the realm of
magic.

We moved forward again. Still more passages, more footprints—and another lake. These subterranean pools are especially uncanny. Their waters lie very still. No breath of
air ever ruffles them. If you throw your lamp's light upon
the surface, it seems black, solid even. The absolute immo-
bility appears so unnatural, so incredible, that one cannot
resist some feeling of apprehension.

A lake full of dread—and unreal.

More traces of Ice Age Man. One can make out the imprints of the heels, the balls of the feet, the toes.

By now we had been almost two hours in the innermost
recesses of a mountain. We had been wandering about,
crawling, sliding, clambering . . . now the cave veered toward the left. The vault became low again; still there was
a clearance of about six feet. Then, without any warning,
we were in the last chamber, the celebrated Hall of Bisons.

We could not suppress a cry. The Bison Sculptures. Each
beast is about two feet long as we see it by the flickering
light of our lamps. These sculptures are no primitive carvings, they are works of surprising plastic beauty, filled with
an astounding force of expression and rich with indwelling
life. The nearer of the two animals is a cow and behind
her stands the bull just about to mount. Obviously a piece
of fertility magic. Bisons, we may remember, had come to

be rather rare beasts in Magdalenian times, so there was every inducement to enchant them that they might multiply.

All around the sculptures, traces of men. We lift up one of the footprint-casts from the ground. They consist of nothing but heel-marks, only heels; and heels, moreover, of young men, of lads, say about thirteen or fourteen years old. And it is marvelous how clear the grooves and marks of the skin are.

These things raise a whole host of questions in one's mind. Why only heels? Why only the heels of children? Since there are no other imprints than those of heels, it is obvious that this must have been a dance-floor, used for some sort of cult-dance. A cult-dance around the figures of bisons, the fertility-magic sculptures. We may ask ourselves if this could not have been a bison-dance. I am inclined to think that it was and that the dancers wore bison-horns as they stamped and strode as though they were hoofed. In the dance, the dancers were bisons and wore bisons' disguises. There came into my mind an eagle-dance I had seen among American Indians. In this all the performers *were* eagles; they had been transformed into eagles and fluttered about as the great birds do.

But then, why a dance for children only? Well, among all so-called "primitive" peoples, or among nearly all, at any rate, there occur, at a certain stage in life, great festivals—there is a faint and pale reflection of these in the Christian confirmation rites. At these great festivities children are received into the society of the tribe. They are admitted as full-grown adults, men and women. In the case of hunting peoples, the neophytes are then allowed to hunt with their fathers, while with all such peoples the young are initiated into the mysteries of adult life. The boys and girls behold the marvels of fertility and fecundity, of the beginning of life, of the commencement of each individual's being—the greatest of wonders.

We followed the traces, the footprints. These lead to the rock walls and they lead to five different spots. Everywhere we found phallic engravings, symbols of life, birth, beginning. More magic, in this last and most remote of the grottoes hidden in the belly of a mountain.

Without saying a word, Louis directed us toward a certain part of the walls. Sticking in it was an Ice Age stone knife. With such an instrument, doubtless, the wizard of the tribe carved the enchanted bisons. Then, one day, men forsook this chamber; they abandoned, maybe, the whole cave. The very existence of this sanctuary was forgotten and it was never again visited, either in prehistoric or later times, until, after the passage of millennia, Louis and his two brothers penetrated right into the heart of palaeolithic mysteries.

One can hardly help reflecting upon the chain of descent that reaches down to us from our distant ancestors of Old Stone Age times . . . ten thousand years at least, ten thousand years of endurance, and, it must be admitted, of great good luck . . . sobering thoughts . . . the endless succession of births and deaths throughout the ages.

We moved up, once again, to examine the sculptures more closely. They were modeled from the clay of the cavern itself. The great withers of the bulls are powerfully arched, his muzzle is shoved forward, his little sharp horns stand out against his ears, the mighty legs are taut. The tension of the body, as it prepares to spring, is depicted with admirable clarity, while the mane and the hair below the muzzle of the cow-bison are particularly well rendered.

As the lamp's light plays upon the sculpture, the shadows flit ghostlike about the figures. So must the beasts have appeared to Ice Age Man when, with his lamps, he penetrated into the holy heart of the mountain.

There is also a third sculpture of a bison, but it is much smaller than the other two and not so impressive.

Then, at last, we dragged ourselves away from the sanctuary. With one last look we embraced the sculptures, the telltale traces of the magic dance.

We began a long tramp back through the grottoes. Once again we had to squeeze through the "cat's hole," and still once more we must make our way through narrow passages and galleries. When we had followed the course of the Volp and our boat had shot out through the low entrance, it was already quite dark. We had spent a whole day, nearly twelve hours, in the shrines of prehistoric men.

That evening, as we sat round the fire at the Château de Pujol, the talk, naturally, turned upon caves and especially upon the Tuc d'Audoubert and the impression this had made on us. Presently, Count Bégouen got up and brought us some objects found during the excavations made at the entrance to the cavern.

"These were discovered in the hall, you know what I mean, in the lower part of the cavern, before you get to the 'chimney' with the steps cut in it. As far as can be seen this was the only part of the Tuc d'Audoubert where men ever lived. Two Magdalenian strata were revealed; the one separated from the other by a sterile layer. From this it is clear that Magdalenian-culture Ice Age families made their homes there at two different periods. We dug up these pieces last summer, no one knows about them yet and they have not been published."

And he laid in my hand some small carvings of horses' heads and a stone engraved with the likeness of a bison.

"This last piece has a peculiar history. On June 18, 1914, that's to say less than two months before war broke out, Professor Birkner of Munich came here to see the cave and the bison sculptures. He and I, and one of my students, went off by boat into the cavern. When we had visited the grottoes and wanted to get out again, we found that, during the day, the Volp's level had risen. It had been raining a lot, and there was no space left between the surface of the water and the vault of the entrance tunnel. There was no hope of getting the boat through so we had just to stay in the cave. We waited the whole evening but the level did not go down. We realized that we should have to spend the whole night underground. We lay down in a corner of the lower chamber, but it was very damp, water was trickling down the walls and we had neither rugs nor blankets. So we decided, more to keep ourselves warm than for any other reason, to do some digging. We had only just grabbed our spades when Birkner found this stone. He dipped it in the water and then let out a shout of delight. He'd seen the engraving. The next day, by about noon, the Volp's level had dropped and we were able to get out of the cave again."

VI: Les Trois-Frères

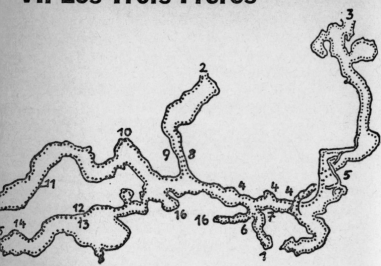

Ground plan of Les Trois-Frères Cavern, near Montesquieu-Avantès, Ariège Department, France: (*1*) Original entrance. (*2*) Present entrance. (*3*) Entrance to the Enlène Cave. (*4*) Site of excavations. (*5*) Drop down to the River Volp. (*6*) Painting of horse. (*7*) Engravings. (*8*) Painting in black pigment: Bison. (*9*) Hands. (*10*) Dots. (*11*) Dots. (*12*) Engravings: Lions. (*13*) Bison skeleton. (*14*) Hall of Pictures. (*15*) The Wizard. (*16*) Unexplored passage.

And now you must see Les Trois-Frères as well," said Count Bégouen to me one morning as we sat at breakfast on the terrace of the Château de Pujol. This was just what I had been hoping he would say.

"Louis will be free all day tomorrow and he's told me that he'll be delighted to go with you, although his work hardly allows him to take so much time off—for you have to reckon a whole day for the excursion."

"I don't know how to thank you for all your kindness

. . . for me a visit to Les Trois-Frères is of the greatest importance . . . it's really not possible to talk intelligently about prehistoric pictures, paintings and sculpture, if one hasn't seen them for oneself."

"Professor van Giffen from Groningen, in Holland, is coming to see us today and we'll take him with us on our outing."

That afternoon we went off to see the famous Mas d'Azil cave—from which the name "Azilian" was derived. It is applied to the culture-period which followed on after the end of the Magdalenian . . . in fact the Azilian is the first of the post-glacial cultures. Excavation began at Mas d'Azil as long ago as 1876 and has been going on, more or less, ever since. Many of the best-known prehistoric works of art were discovered at this site, which comprises several strata of Magdalenian and then, above them, Azilian and, over that, Neolithic.

The cave is enormous. It is, indeed, more an immense tunnel, or passage, than a cavern in the ordinary use of the word, and the high road runs right through the grotto. We left our car in the interior of the cavern, by the side of the road, and climbed up to the excavations which lie quite close to the thoroughfare. We had brought spades with us and began a trial dig in a hitherto untouched part of the site. It was not long before we got down to the Magdalenian layers and we were soon holding in our hands stone and bone artifacts, scrapers and knives, arrowheads and a harpoon. Then, when we examined the surface of former excavations, I came across a painted Azilian pebble.

"Some more digging ought to be done here," said Bégouen, "it looks very promising; much of this rather large area has not been touched at all. But such things cost money and take a long time."

"But I do hope you'll think about further digging. It would be very well worth while for someone to get really busy here."

And, later on, Count Bégouen did think about it. From

1937 on, further excavations were undertaken, many art-objects were recovered and, moreover, a new gallery was discovered, a side-passage whose existence had been totally unsuspected. From this gallery no less than four subsidiary corridors branch off and two of them are adorned with numerous pictures. In 1949 I was lucky enough to be able to visit the new grottoes and to examine their paintings, but of course in 1926 there was no question of anything like that.

On our way back to Pujol we talked about Les Trois-Frères.

Count Bégouen told us the story of the discovery.

"The circumstances were very extraordinary," he began. I was sitting beside him and can see his impressive figure now. A Basque beret was on his head, his full white beard flowed in the wind and his eyes sparkled. He spoke with much animation, for he is full of inner fire and temperament. And his French is more elegant than one hears very often nowadays.

"It was on the eve of the 1914 war, July 20, 1914, to be precise. The date is forever fixed in my memory because it was the second anniversary of the discovery of the Tuc d'Audoubert. The weather was marvelous, so wonderful, indeed, that we decided to take a day off. It was to be a birthday party for the Tuc d'Audoubert. We made all our preparations the evening before, the luncheon baskets were packed, the lamps trimmed and checked up, our cave-clothes laid out. Early in the morning we set off. It was very hot indeed. The sun blazed down from a pitiless sky and we hadn't gone very far before we felt we had to take a rest. We were on a grassy down, or slope, that reached up obliquely along the side of the mountain. There were very few trees about and the few there were didn't cast much shade. It was then that we met a peasant walking down the hill. He recognized us at once, and when he learned that we were looking for somewhere cool to sit he suggested that we should go to what he called *le trou souffleur*, or the 'blow hole.' There, he assured us, it was cool on even the hottest summer days because a slight, fresh breeze always arose out of the earth. I had never heard of the place and had no idea where it was, but you may imagine how carefully I listened to the man's story. We followed the peasant's lead and sure enough in a few minutes' time we lit upon the *trou souffleur*. It was surrounded, and also nearly blocked, with stones, but we pushed our hands inside the *trou* and, there was no doubt about it, a cool current of air was blowing from inside the bowels of the hill. We cleared away the stones, flattened the earth and then began to dig. When the hole was big enough for us to peer down into it, it seemed to lead on a long way, but it was, of course, so black that we couldn't see very much or very far. Therefore, naturally, we went on working to enlarge the aperture. It was terrifically hot and our sweat ran down in great trickles to the earth, but our curiosity was too much for us. When the opening was about three feet broad we saw that we'd need a rope, for the drop was sheer inside. Therefore, we borrowed a clothesline from a neighboring cottage and with that we let down one of my sons with the rope tied round his body, but as he slithered down he kept on knocking against the sides of the pit, which seemed to have no bottom . . . forty feet, fifty feet, sixty feet . . . then we felt he'd struck bottom and was untying himself. He'd taken a ball of string with him as a precaution so that, like Theseus in the Labyrinth, he might find his way back again safely.

"We sat down and waited. It had been agreed that the boy who'd gone down should come back as soon as possible and tell us what he'd found. But he didn't come back. We waited patiently for the first fifteen minutes. During the second quarter of an hour we began to get a little anxious, and when nearly three-quarters of an hour had passed we started to discuss what we ought to do to rescue the boy imprisoned down there below. As a matter of fact we didn't get any sign till more than an hour had gone by.

When we'd got the lad up to the surface again you can imagine how relieved and pleased we were.

"His face was red with excitement, and he could hardly speak when he emerged from the *trou souffleur*. Once he was beside us he kept on hanging round my neck and crying for joy while he shouted, 'It's a quite new cave, there's pictures, pictures, hundreds of them!' . . . and we were all so excited and worked up that we quite forgot about the Tuc d'Audoubert and our plans . . . the new cave filled our minds and fired our imaginations while my son told us about narrow passages, huge halls, and marvelous pictures.

"Then we all went down, one after the other, and when we stood below we couldn't resist shouting aloud for joy and delight. There and then we baptized the new grotto 'Les Trois-Frères,' after 'The Three Brothers,' my three sons."

Bégouen's face lit up as he told his story; he had taken off his beret and wisps of hair were blowing all around his face.

"It's such a pity," I said, "that up to now almost nothing has been published about Les Trois-Frères. The cave was discovered quite a number of years ago, yet we have hardly any idea of what the Trois-Frères pictures look like."

"Publication would present enormous difficulties; it would, indeed, be almost impossible. Most of the pictures are on a sheer wall-surface, high above the ground, and the drawings lie inextricably mixed up one over another; there are three hundred at least, perhaps five hundred of them— all engravings, drawings."

"No paintings, no color?"

"No, none, except for the famous shaman, the Wizard himself. All the other figures are drawings. But tomorrow you'll see for yourself—and when you've seen for yourself I know what you're going to say; you'll tell me that Les Trois-Frères is one of the finest, the most important, and the most significant of all prehistoric caves."

By this time we had got back to the Château de Pujol.

Van Giffen had arrived while we were away. When we had dined we went out again on to the terrace. . . .

The next day we made a very early start, Louis Bégouen, van Giffen, and we two. Bégouen's little dog ran after us for a time . . . then he tired and fell back, barking.

"We've got another entrance now," said Louis Bégouen. "We don't have to drop down sixty feet any more. That was altogether too much of a good thing. We found a communicating passage between the Enlène cave and Les Trois-Frères and now we use the Enlène entrance for both. Still, you'll have to crawl along on your bellies for at least fifty yards, that can't be avoided."

After about an hour's walking we got to the entrance. It is very inconspicuous and hard to find, for it is more than half-hidden in scrub and bushes. We lighted our lamps and then went inside.

"Still fewer people have visited Les Trois-Frères than the Tuc d'Audoubert. Up to now only eight archaeologists. Breuil comes here every year and makes some drawings for a big book on the cave, but there are too many of them. As a matter of fact, he's been copying the engravings for years and still he's nowhere near finished."

Soon we came up to a spot where there was a stratum that had yielded a number of objects. We dug a little and soon had collected a number of engraved stones and some carvings.

Now we could walk upright, and we followed each other in Indian file, our lamps swaying as we held them at arm's length. The ground was markedly damp and slimy, so we had to exercise a good deal of care not to slip upon the very irregular floor. We walked upward and we walked downward and then we came to a very narrow passage, some ten or twelve yards long, where we had to crawl on all fours. After that, more chambers and constricted corridors. In one large room there are numerous red and black blobs or dots, but nothing in the way of pictures—just these dots.

The stalactites were splendid. Water dropped softly from the ceiling. No other sound could be heard and there was no movement to be perceived anywhere. We sat down on some boulders and ate a few sandwiches.

Such complete silence is uncanny. We seemed to be already far into the heart of the mountain and completely isolated from the outer world. We all rebel instinctively against the overpowering sensation of the past, we refuse to accept a state of things where everything we regard as important is seen to be without permanence. But it is impossible not to wonder about the fate of the men who came this way ten thousand years ago. They were, no doubt, our ancestors. . . . If there are about three generations to a century, then there must be thirty in a millennium . . . ten thousand years is three hundred generations ago. Three hundred male and three hundred female forebears one behind the other. It is difficult to imagine that, or indeed to measure in any way what a span of ten thousand years can be.

The drops of water fall continuously, regularly, always at the same interval. You feel that they must forever thus have fallen and that they will, in like manner, fall to all eternity. It will always be quite still here even if above and outside men fight and love, build up or tear down.

We set off again. Across the long, spacious hall to the tunnel. We put our lamps down on the ground and then push them forward into the low burrow. Louis led, after him came van Giffen, then Rita, while I brought up the rear. The passage was not much wider than the breadth of my shoulders—and not any higher than broad. Ahead of me I could hear the others groaning while their lamps moved forward very slowly. We held our arms close to our bodies and, just as in the Tuc d'Audoubert "cat's hole" or *chattière*, we slithered forward like snakes upon our bellies. And this Trois-Frères passage is much harder going than the Tuc d'Audoubert *chattière*. In places it is only a foot high, so that one must lay one's face right on the earth. It is like creeping through a coffin. You cannot raise your head, you can hardly breathe . . . at last, the burrow gets slightly higher, you can bear down a little on your fore-arms and pull your head up a little also. But this relief does not last long. Again the way narrows and lowers. You

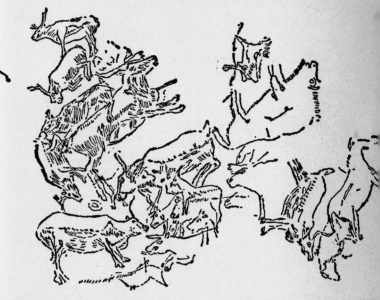

Portion of wall engravings in the Trois-Frères Cavern near Montesquieu-Avantès, Ariège Department, France. Mid-Mag-dalenian. One-tenth actual size.

have to push painfully forward, inch by inch, foot by foot.

No one spoke. We kept our lamps a few inches before us and dragged ourselves after them. Ahead of me I could hear the others moaning with the strain.

Your heart throbs distressingly. Breathing becomes an al-most unbearable effort.

It was terrible to have the roof so close to one's head, and as it is a very hard, rocky roof, I kept knocking my head against the stony bumps and bosses. Then, quite sud-denly, we got through and out. We all breathed deeply once more and felt as though we had been rescued from some mortal danger.

We were standing in a colossal hall. We threw our lamp-light up toward the roof and then along the walls. An enormous place. And here, at last, were the drawings. From top to bottom a whole wall is covered with engravings. The

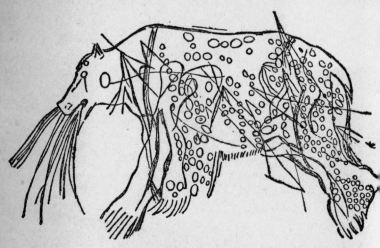

Engraving of a bear riddled with arrows: Mid-Magdalenian. One-third actual size. Trois-Frères Cavern, near Montesquieu-Avantès, Ariège Department, France.

drawings were cut onto the rock-face by means of stone knives, and now one can see marshaled here the beasts that lived in southwestern France thousands and thousands of years ago: mammoth and rhinoceros, bison, wild horse, bear, wild ass and reindeer, glutton, musk-ox. There are even small beasts not often to be seen upon the walls of prehistoric caverns: snowy owls, hares—fish, even. And here and there, scattered about, are arrows aimed and directed at the animals. Several pictures of bears are especially noteworthy, since these creatures are shown as wounded while blood pours from their muzzles. Real sporting prints, hunting pictures, a presentment of the magic of the chase.

The animals are depicted in the most natural and vivid manner. No modern artist can do anything better—or even as good. The outlines are quite lightly indicated and in no case has there been retouching. Sometimes the contours are quite loose, line is laid near line until the outline appears almost fluid. In fact, these Trois-Frères drawings are delicate, full of imagination and so free in form that they can be compared only with the work of the French Impressionists. The Ice Age artists, at Les Trois-Frères, show also that they had studied the problems presented by the representation of full-face, front views. There is a lion that seems to stare at the onlooker . . . and two snowy owls as seen from the front. And everything, every drawing and design the eye lights upon, appears natural, full of life, real.

There is a sorcerer playing the flute before two beasts. There is another shaman clad in a bison's fell . . . and then, high up, more than ten feet above the ground, the famed Wizard of Les Trois-Frères himself. This figure was already, at the time of our visit, well known from many reproductions, but all the other drawings in the cavern were unknown and, in those days at least, none of them had been published.

The Wizard is the most singular and striking figure in the whole cave. Engraved above the other pictures—and it is hardly fanciful to imagine that they may all be from one hand—the Wizard may well have depicted himself as the protector of the whole assemblage. It is difficult to understand how the artist reached this spot about twelve feet above the ground, but get there he did, for the painting exists to prove that somehow or other the painter was able to hoist himself up to execute his picture. In this portrait, alone of all the Trois-Frères pictures, pigment is used, black paint to supplement the engraving.

The Wizard's great round eyes stare out in sinister, even frightening, fashion. This man of the Ice Age gazes right at us. There are very few pictures I know of which convey such an impression, which exercise such power over the beholder. Through the millennia the Wizard stared into emptiness, until men in our days came again to meet his glance.

It is a human body with human thigh, knee, calf, and foot, and it dances, one foot pushed forward and the other raised, both legs flexed at the knees. The magician in his

Engraving of cave lion (felis spelaea) *seen from front: Mid-Magdalenian. One-quarter actual size. Trois-Frères Cavern, near Montesquieu-Avantès, Ariège Department, France.*

magic dance. But he bears no human visage. He wears a stag-mask with wide, spreading antlers and his long, pointed beard reaches halfway down his chest. His hands are hidden beneath bear's paws while from his buttocks trails the tail of a wild horse. The upper part of the body is bent forward, the hands slightly raised and curved downward. And he is dancing. Dancing the beast-dance, and as he dances he stares steadfastly with his great round, unblinking eyes.

The painting, indeed, is uncanny and arresting. We lingered long before it and before the great wall of drawings. At last we realized that we must turn and make our way back. Once again we must slide painfully through the coffin-like burrow, once again wriggle through on our bellies . . . the long, almost endless way back to the outer world.

We staggered out of the cavern. When we got into the open it was still light. We were giddy. You cannot so quickly get used to light, to the day, to life as we live it.

Wizard playing flute and enchanting beasts. Mid-Magdalenian. One-third actual size. Trois-Frères Cavern near Montesquieu-Avantès, Ariège Department, France.

We had emerged from eternity into mortality. Unaltering, changeless were the halls, the passages, the dripping waters, the unswerving gaze of the Wizard high up above his world of pictures. Compared with these things, what we could see around us—trees, woods, meadows, men themselves—seemed almost illusions.

We made our way slowly home again. Like the fairy stories . . . you know what I mean. A man comes back from the eternal realms. A girl falls into a spring, a fountain. She finds a meadow set with beautiful trees, a castle, a prince . . . and then the magic fades. . . . She is back where she was.

That is what we felt like after our visit to Les Trois-Frères and when the day was all around us. Between the eternal and the ephemeral, each most difficult to comprehend, there seems to be no point of contact, so when we see them together they arouse in us either anxiety or terror.

Wizard in garments made of beasts' skins. Actual size 2 feet. From a drawing by H. Breuil. Trois-Frères Cavern, near Montesquieu-Avantès, Ariège Department, France.

VII: Cabrerets

Ground plan of the Marsoulas Cave, near Saliès-du-Salat, Haute-Garonne Department, France: (1) Entrance. (2) Excavation site (Bégouen, Russell). (3) Excavation site (Regnault). (4) Excavation site (Cau-Durban). (5) Paintings and engravings. (6) Subterranean stream.

We were clambering about and crouching our way through the Marsoulas cavern near Saliès-du-Salat in the Haute-Garonne department of southwestern, of Pyrenean, France. It was in 1931 and I had taken some students on a prehistoric pilgrimage. We had made our way as far as possible by motor-bus, and then we had had a hard job finding our bearings; in fact, until one of the villagers kindly guided us, we did not know where we were. Finally, however, we got to the cavern that has become so important in the history of prehistoric painting and of its revelation.

The cave is low-vaulted and quite short while the walls both to right and left are covered with paintings almost from top to bottom. One would think that it was quite impossible for anyone in the cavern to overlook the pictures, yet the Abbé Cau-Durban, vicar of Saint-Girons, dug here almost daily during the years from 1881 to 1884 and appears to have taken no notice of the paintings. He published a whole series of papers on Marsoulas but in them he made no mention at all of any frescoes. Quite close to one of the rock walls he turned up a piece of bone engraved with the figure of a bison. It seems to us, now at all events, quite a natural thing to conclude that Ice Age men might well have executed the big paintings upon the cave walls as well as the little bits of decorated bone (which, after all, had to be looked for in the earth); moreover, the Marsoulas pictures, like those of Altamira, indeed, were there staring any visitor in the face. However, the archaeological vicar never seems to have made any such deductions from the objects he discovered in Magdalenian and Solutrean strata which he cleared very carefully and examined very thoroughly.

After Cau-Durban, another excavator, one Félix Regnault, worked at Marsoulas. He at least, as we know, did notice the paintings, but he did not consider them ancient. That was in 1897. No doubt, such was the prevalent opinion in those days that Regnault did not dare to regard the pictures as authentically prehistoric and very ancient. He made no mention of them except in private letters to scientific acquaintances or to friends. It was not until 1902 (when the large and very important caves of Font-de-Gaume and Les Combarelles were discovered) that Regnault ventured to publish in a scientific journal an article on the Marsoulas pictures. In this same year, 1902, Cartailhac and Breuil visited the cavern. The pictures were copied and, in 1905, published.

So for a whole generation, for a period of no less than thirty years, archaeologists dug at Marsoulas and made important excavations. Every day these men saw the pictures, yet no one dared to take them for works of remote prehistoric date. After all, there existed nothing similar, noth-

Engraved rock wall. Late Aurignacian. One-twentieth actual size. Cabrerets Cavern, Department of the Lot, France.

ing comparable (Altamira had been forgotten)—it was, perhaps, as though a piece of classical Greek sculpture had been dug out of the earth and exhibited to a world in which no one knew anything about Greece or had ever seen or heard of a Greek work of art. There was no means of "situating" these strange wall-paintings and therefore, of course, they could not be understood.

My students were fascinated by the Marsoulas pictures and they would vie with one another in discovering details and peculiarities. We were all peering into the strange human caricatures on the walls, things both sinister and comic . . . shamans, wizards, magicians wearing beast-masks . . . then we heard a car pull up on the road. . . . Our driver, who had come into the cave with us, stepped out to see what was happening, and probably also to keep an eye on his bus. A lady and a gentleman were walking up the slope to the cavern. I at once recognized him as Passemard, the well-known excavator of the Isturitz cave not very far from Biarritz. I had known him for some years and when we were excavating together at Isturitz I was

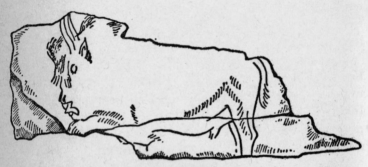

Bison: Engraving on bone. Actual size. Marsoulas Cave, Haute-Garonne Department, France.

often a guest in his house. After a cordial greeting we set to work with him to examine the Marsoulas pictures. It was a very lucky chance that brought us together that day, for we were able to discuss many of the problems of cave art while we were standing in front of original paintings.

"Don't you think it's quite easy to recognize," I asked him, "that these pictures date from mid-Magdalenian times? Just look at this loosening of line; no real outlines to be seen; all the essence of the picture is in perspective, in plastic quality, in the impression it gives of volume and space."

"Of course, it's unmistakable and, by the way, Cau-Dur-ban found here evidence of a fine mid-Magdalenian culture whose engraved bone-fragments showed precisely the same

style as that of the frescoes. The finest of the Cau-Durban
pieces is a figure of a bison and this can be found again,
on a large scale, on the walls."

We moved on from picture to picture scrutinizing everything in detail.

"Look at this one, Passemard, this is the sort of thing
never found except in mid-Magdalenian cultures. The
strokes are free and they do not trace a real outline but
one can sense the joy of the artist in his mastery over form
and contour. When I look at this I feel he must have been
quite proud that he didn't need the help of outline any
more, that he could express his artistic imagination quite
freely . . . a whole lot of tiny strokes close together . . .
look . . . and from them the whole picture emerges."

"Just like the modern Impressionistic technique," said
Passemard as he pointed out the different strokes that went
to make up the finished painting. "Just as with our modern
Impressionists, so Ice Age Impressionism was the result of
preceding techniques and traditions. We'll have to creep
along a bit farther and you'll see what I mean."

When we got to about halfway down the cave, there, to
our left, was the figure of a bison executed in strictly
pointillist style. But this painting had outlines, thick outlines
—though executed with a sure enough touch—such as are
characteristic of, and are indeed found only in, late Magdalenian cultures. The great mane of the animal is brought
together into a pointed mass that hangs down—and this
simplification is a hallmark of late Magdalenian technique.

"Just look at this," I said; "isn't it typical of late Magdalenian? And yet, how reminiscent it is of certain later
phases of the Impressionists, say about 1900—I mean the
pointillism. An assemblage of blobs, of dots, more or less
closely grouped together, was employed by artists to in-
tensify the impression of space. . . . Stylistically speaking,
this prehistoric painting is in the same class as a work by
Signac or Seurat."

"I agree with that," replied Passemard. "I'd never made

Pointillist paintings: Mid-Magdalenian. Dimensions of bison on left: 3 feet. Marsoulas Cavern, near Saliès-du-Salat, Haute-Garonne Department, France.

the comparison before, but I can see it clear enough now."

"What about this one here to the right? A horse; the outline is strongly and clearly marked and it is, moreover, quite without interruption or discontinuity. That sort of thing, I think, was never done in mid-Magdalenian times . . . it's definitely late Magdalenian. Firm, bold, assured outlines, and the shading powerful, almost aggressive. And, here again, we've got more pointillism. . . ."

"At Isturitz," added Passemard, "in the latest Magdalenian, that is to say Magdalenian VI, I unearthed a few engravings showing just this same sort of stroke. There's one drawing on stone that depicts a horned animal, but the antlers are so schematized—the tendency toward schematization is, as you know, a feature of the latest Magdalenian —that it is impossible to identify the beast for certain. In that late period it would seem that a broad, subjective, almost slap-dash technique was a characteristic of the artists."

"It seems to me," I said, turning to Passemard, "that the problem of the development of styles is a very crucial one. If we've been right in our opinion about the evolution of late palaeolithic art, then it seems to me that in this development we can find an exemplar, a pattern, as it were, for all the later trends in artistic creation. Here, in Marsoulas, we've got fine examples of the prehistoric artistic apogee, that of mid-Magdalenian times, as well as specimens of late Magdalenian painting. That is to say, the former 'Impressionistic' and the latter characterized by what we've called the 'slap-dash' technique. In these conditions the most ancient pictorial art must surely have been one of simple

Deep-line engraving of a bison: Aurignacian. One-fifth actual size. La Grèze, near Les Eyzies, Dordogne Department, France.

lines . . . an outline, but executed less boldly, with less assurance, more tentatively. Wölfflin it was, I think, who spoke about 'linear' and 'picturesque' art. He's quite right. The artistic evolution in Renaissance times, for instance, takes this path from the 'linear' to the 'picturesque.'

"And the movement from the late Impressionists to the Expressionists is one in the other sense, from the 'picturesque' back again to the 'linear.' So, I'm inclined to hold that Ice Age art must have been first of all 'linear,' then 'picturesque,' and then again 'linear.' Here at Marsoulas we've got the 'picturesque' and the later 'linear' phases well represented. Where do we go to find the earlier 'linear' forms?"

And all the time we went on creeping about from picture to picture. The cave is not only very narrow but is also low-vaulted, so that most of the time one has to crawl about on one's hands and knees. You are liable to get a bad headache from not being able ever to stand upright. And then again, on this day there were far too many of us in the cave at one time. We kept on barging into each other while trying to avoid brushing the pictures with our clothes. It is a very good thing that an iron grating closes the cavern's entrance and that only those really interested in prehistoric art can gain admittance.

But we could find nowhere any examples of the paintings of the earliest phases.

"There's no doubt about it," said Passemard, "you'll have to go to Cabrerets, that's the place where you'll get a splendid idea of Aurignacian art and, indeed, of all the earlier styles and techniques."

"That would be quite an undertaking; it would demand, at least, two whole days . . . and we'd have to get hold of a car. . . ." Then I began making rapid calculations to see if we would have enough money to go around if we all went.

"Cabrerets is a must," went on Passemard, "and I'd be delighted to come with you. It's the classical site for the earlier phases of prehistoric pictorial art."

"Maybe, then, we could manage it, and it would be marvelous if you could come too. Cabrerets will just round off and complete our prehistoric pilgrimage."

"Cabrerets was discovered in 1922," explained Passemard. "It was a fourteen-year-old boy who found the grotto while he was playing in the woods. As his name was David, the place is often called the 'David Cave' after him, but its most usual name is Pech Merle; that is, 'Blackbird Hill.'"

Then we got to discussing all sorts of plans and projects. Finally we decided that, the next day, we would take the

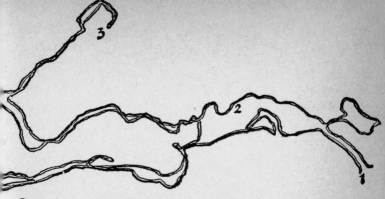

*Ground plan of the Pech-Merle Cavern, Cabrerets, Lot Depart-
ment, France. (1) Existing entrance. (2) Hall with pictures.
(3) Former entrance.*

train to the station nearest Cabrerets and then go on by
car. In the train, by great good chance, we met the Comte
de Saint-Périer, a well-known French archaeologist who
excavated the Lespugue cave. It was he, indeed, who discovered the famed female statuette of Lespugue. I had
known him for long and had, on several occasions, been his
guest at his country house, the Château de Morigny, near
Etampes, to the southwest of Paris. There we had spent
days, Madame de Saint-Périer, our host and myself, in
examining the objects from his excavations: cases full of
harpoons, of burins and scrapers, other cases with blades;
in short, an inexhaustible collection of objects which the
Saint-Périers had dug up. Later, he continued Passemard's
work at Isturitz and there, also, his luck was remarkable.
He would show me ever more and more art-objects, engravings on stone and bone, carvings . . . horses' heads,
bisons, and human figures. For days on end we would
discuss the nature of late palaeolithic art, new discoveries,
recent excavations, all sorts of problems and possibilities of
research. I was delighted to see him again and we went
along to the dining-car where we drank a toast to our
common investigations into the origins of human cultures!

M. de Saint-Périer was going on to Paris so we left him in the train, hired a car, and made off for Cabrerets. The cavern is about two miles away from Cabrerets village and on the rising ground that is known as the "Pech Merle," which is in the dale of a rivulet known as the Sagne.

Our luck held that day because, before we got to the cave, we encountered the explorer of the whole region, the Abbé Lemozi, who was the cave's good genius and protector in the early years after its discovery. Now an entrance has been erected and this leads to steps going down into the cave. Walls have been cemented. Massive iron doors protect the cave itself. Inside the cavern much of the water-borne sand has been dug away to make room for paths and passages paved and consolidated with cement. Railings have been placed to prevent visitors from touching the pictures; in fact, Cabrerets is a remarkably pleasant cave to visit.

When it was first discovered, the aperture leading into the cave was almost entirely blocked with stalagmites which had to be removed before exploration of the interior could be undertaken. That was in August, 1922.

The most important pictures are to be found in a huge hall more than a hundred yards long. There are some forty figures of animals, in part painted, in part engraved. The pictures begin as soon as you get into the grottoes: a whole series of mammoths, reindeer, horses, some under others, some over others, and all in an excellent state of preservation. On the vaults and ceilings are scratchings made with human fingers and some of these depict men wearing beast-masks. Two further chambers open out of the main hall. These also contain paintings and engravings—cave bears, wild horses, mammoths.

We moved about from picture to picture. We talked and discussed color, draughtsmanship, techniques. Pech Merle is by no means so uncanny a cave as many others. It resembles, rather, an immense hall from which a few lateral passages lead off. The existing entrance, however, is certainly not the one used in palaeolithic times. That was somewhere else and has not yet been found, though it is clear that, in Ice Age times, men must have entered the cave through the lateral passages leading to the main hall adorned with frescoes. As was the case with Altamira and Lascaux, the main hall was the first part to be seen by the discoverers and, also at Altamira and at Lascaux, as at Pech Merle, the original entrances have not yet been found and may well be buried and quite inaccessible.

The Cabrerets grottoes excited my imagination more and more with the problems of style-change in Old Stone Age art. What could be the appearance of the very beginnings of what became the highly developed Ice Age pictorial art?

"Just look here, Kühn; for one thing, those pictures there must be late in date since they lie on the top of the others, while those over there must be much older, the oldest perhaps, since they are just formed of finger-scratches."

We walked along to where we could examine the vaulting and then stood for a long while gazing at the strange scratches that are so hard to distinguish, for they seem to move and squirm and wriggle under and over each other. Lemozi furnished us with several of his own explanations . . . it is true that you can make out figures of men and also figures of women, but how the actual lines run it is difficult to say. They mingle, touch, and merge into one another.

"Here you are," announced Passemard, "here's the beginning of representational art. Here it's easy enough to see how men—and they must have been men of Aurignacian culture, too—imitated the claw-marks of the cave bears. Just as the bears tore with their claws so did late Old Stone Age men with their nails scratch lines on the soft limestone walls. Look here, for instance, one can easily make out the traces of the three middle fingers."

"And that's just like the marks at La Clotilde de Santa Isabel, near Torrelavega in the Cantabrian region of northern Spain, or at Hornos de la Peña in the same district, at La Pileta in southern Spain down near Gibraltar, or at Gargas, here in France, in the Haute-Garonne department. Just scratches, pretty certainly imitated from those of the great carnivores. Still, this stage of scratching and scoring and scraping does not seem to have lasted very long. Soon outlines of animals appear. Both at Altamira and Hornos de la Peña, pictures of early Magdalenian technique occur over simple scratchings which are, therefore, quite obviously older. But I think we can say that man created something —even if it was in imitation of wild beasts' claw-marks— by scoring the cave walls and then by staining his hands and sticking them against the rock-faces; both these acts aroused the idea of artistic creation, of the possibility of making what we call 'art.' "

"But how long has the use of color been known?" one of the students asked me.

"Well, that's hard to say, but Neanderthaloid men may have painted their bodies; anyway, red ochre occurs on Neanderthaloid remains, such as those of La Chapelle-aux-Saints (in the Corrèze department) and the two skeletons from La Ferrassie in the Dordogne. If, indeed, Neanderthaloid men understood the use of color, then there's no wonder that the physically more refined 'modern' type of men also employed it; that is to say, the men who were the authors of the art we see around us."

"So, if it was familiarity with the use of pigments, and marks made in imitation of animals' claw-scratches, that brought men to the conception of representational art, then things were more or less as Herder maintained," put in another student.

"Yes, I think you're right," I replied. "Herder saw a long way into the problem and, essentially, his idea was just. A philosopher nearer to us in time, Theodor Lipps, has developed a whole theory of aesthetics which reposes upon the idea of empathy. According to his theory, the spiritual content of art is due to empathy through which the inanimate becomes animate, and the animate is projected into the inanimate. And this theory applies perhaps to the very beginning of art. At Les Combarelles there's a bulge on the rock surface, a quite natural formation, but it does bear some resemblance to an animal form, and this natural shape was supplemented by art; those parts of the body which were lacking were supplied by means of engraving. In the same cavern there's another rock protuberance. It looks rather like a man's nose. By empathy men were led to complete nature's work, by the addition of nostrils and eyes. In the Covalanas cave, again, there's a bit of rock that reminds one of the back of some beast. To this natural formation the Ice Age artist added head, forelegs, belly, and hind legs. At Niaux, also, there's a bulge shaped like an animal. A few strokes of paint developed the figure; brought out, so to speak, the latent form. So it's really imaginative insight—in the earliest phases of art as in the later periods—it's imaginative insight that gives rise to, that encourages, artistic activity."

The Abbé Lemozi, who had been listening to what I said, added: "Quite near Cabrerets there's a cave that was discovered in 1920. It's called Marcenac. There, also, there's a natural bulge in the rock-face . . . a few strokes of dark paint . . . and hey presto! there's a bison."

"I think we can agree that here at Cabrerets, for instance, we come right up against the very beginnings of art upon this earth," put in Passemard while I summarized my thoughts on the subject.

"After these humble beginnings such as we can see here, art developed, representational art evolved in simple outlines. Aurignacian art, for instance, is just this, an art of outlines, of simple linear enclosures. A number of examples illustrate this. For instance, in the Pair-non-Pair cave (Gironde department) there are such outline drawings, sharply drawn outlines without any strokes at all within the bounding lines. And these drawings certainly belong to the early Aurignacian—or at the least to the middle Aurignacian.

That's quite certain, for these things first came to light when the cave's stratum of upper Aurignacian filling was removed. There are, as a matter of fact, a good many other examples. At La Grèze (Dordogne department) there's a magnificent picture of a bison which became visible only after the removal of the Solutrean levels that entirely covered the figure. Such cases allow of unquestionable dating to Aurignacian culture-phases, and we may note that all these undoubtedly Aurignacian pictures consist of simple outlines only."

"It does indeed look as though there is a clearly traceable stylistic current running through Ice Age art," summed up Passemard. "First of all we have the origin of art, largely through empathy—imitation of beasts' claw-scratches and hand-stencils or imprints on walls—then came the development of naturalistic representational art. During the whole of the Aurignacian period the pictures are strictly confined to outlines. In mid-Magdalenian we touched the apogee, the peak of Ice Age art—the facing, and in great measure the solution, of the questions presented by the representation of space and depth, movement and action, of mass, and then such technical problems as the reproduction of fore and rear views. Then, in late Magdalenian times, there appears again the tendency toward simplification, to limitation in fact, to outline-sketches."

"That exactly represents my view," I commented, "and through a whole series of unimpeachably authentic discoveries—on cave walls and of objects recovered from the strata of cave-fillings—this course of stylistic development appears to me to be amply vouched for. And it is obviously of the greatest significance in the history of art, since the same or closely similar courses of development are repeated, time after time, during the ages and as a matter of fact right up to the present time."

We moved on from picture to picture. Cabrerets affords a splendid panorama of the different stages in man's artistic creation. The simple scratches, then the Epoch of Outline.

Over these early things lie, and clearly datable from their superposition, the great paintings of mid-Magdalenian times. Unfortunately, however, at Cabrerets this latter phase is poorly represented and only traces of its paintings can be seen. Nevertheless, the later Magdalenian phases—those when bold contours were once again in favor and were to lead again to outline drawings—are represented by several really good examples in which we have some pointillism as at Marsoulas. In fact the resemblances between some of the Cabrerets pictures and those of Marsoulas are so striking that it is probable there was some artistic contact between the two sites.

The wizard-artists may well have paid visits to their colleagues at times and on such occasions have noticed the work of their fellows. Furthermore, it is most probable that there were real schools that provided an artistic training. It is actually possible to distinguish between various styles and to recognize and pick out, for instance, the art-school of La Laugerie Basse, that of Gourdan, that of Les Combarelles and that of Niaux, to mention no others. In a general way, for any given period, the traditions are comparable and similar, but there are marked differences of detail—just as in our own days. "Impressionism" is a term that covers the work of a whole epoch, but within the framework of the "Impressionist Epoch" the paintings of individual artists are quite clearly distinguishable. It looks as though things were much the same in Ice Age times.

So, gazing, scrutinizing, considering and discussing, we moved from picture to picture. The students, their eyes bright from excitement, stood singly or in little groups before the immensely ancient works of art. Some of the young people were pointing out what struck them most. Others were engaged in animated conversation. We were so oblivious of time and so impressed that we could hardly tear ourselves away from the marvelous masterpieces of prehistoric art.

But, at last, we accepted the Abbé Lemozi's invitation

to go with him to his presbytery and examine his collection of stone artifacts and small art-objects. As soon as he had opened up his cupboards our host displayed before us an unrivaled collection of Ice Age treasures.

On the table were hundreds and hundreds of burins, scrapers, scraping-knives. We were enthralled by the admirable technical skill evidenced by Lemozi's treasures. As one took up the pieces it was a joy to feel how easily the things slipped into one's grip; all little works of art in their way, all alike in style, yet each one subtly different from the other. In those far-off days when the first systematic fabrication of men's tools took place, there was in existence already a kind of standardization. The round scrapers, for instance, are always of the same form, the carene scrapers are always of the same shape. The chipping is of exactly the same character and type; the make of the artifact is, so to speak, regularized. The burins were all worked in the same manner, just as we sharpen a pencil. The points are alike and were produced by a most ingenious and cunning method of striking and chipping. There were instruments which could be used on both sides—combined tools, we might say—a burin on one face and a scraper on the other.

Even the bone implements follow a fixed model. There were awls, bodkins, and harpoons, the latter barbed, at first on one side only and then, later on—in Magdalenian IV and V phases—barbed on both sides. It soon gets quite easy to recognize the different epochs by the techniques employed, as easy as it is for us to tell from the shape and form of table-knives and spoons whether they are Baroque, Rococo, Empire, or "modern style," or whether they are of the latest flat and "functional" types.

Then Lemozi spread out hundreds of sewing-needles before us. We examined many of them. They were wonderfully fine, the points still sharp and the eyes neatly bored. It is astounding how men managed to bore eyes into such thin needles, which were, of course, used to sew the clothing made from animal skins. Since skins were utilized, it is clear that the art of tanning must have been known, for some sort of tanning must have been employed, otherwise the pelts could never have been used for garments.

As the sharp needles passed from hand to hand we wondered more and more at their delicacy, their fine points and the astonishing skill displayed in the fashioning of the eyes. Then, at last, our host took out his collection of art-objects from their cases: engravings on stone and bone, small carvings. An exciting display, with some particularly admirable pieces. The objects were quite small, most of them not longer than one's finger—in fact comparable in size to Japanese netsukes—but, nevertheless, most delicately fashioned and adroitly carved. Some pieces, indeed, were of quite extraordinary beauty. Among the outstanding objects was the engraving of a hind recovered from the Abri Murat, a rock-shelter near Rocamadour in the Lot department. The lines are quite light, yet of remarkable mastery and sureness. Perhaps the most attractive thing about the piece is that the animal is depicted turning her head around to gaze at the beholder. In this way two planes are suggested in a most effective manner. The head, especially, is delicate and soft. The eye, created with a few masterly strokes, is so clear that you feel it is looking at you. Only a very few lines indicate the muzzle but these are so surely drawn, so sharply accentuated, that they alone would suffice to raise the whole picture into the category of undoubted masterpieces.

"Have you got any art-objects from prehistoric sites in Germany?" Lemozi asked me.

"Oh, yes. Art-objects have been found in no less than fourteen different sites. The most important of them are Petersfels near Engen in the Hegau, Thaingen near Schaffhausen. This latter is right on the Swiss border; as a matter of fact, the site is actually in Swiss territory. From Thaingen came an excellent drawing of a grazing reindeer. Then there's Klause near Neuessing, which yielded a drawing of a mammoth. But the most important site of all is Stetten ob Lontal, where there are some very fine Aurignacian carvings."

And all the while Lemozi brought out more and more specimens, which passed from hand to hand—much to our delight. The artistry shown, the successful tackling and solution of a hundred artistic problems . . . we began to feel as though men of the Ice Age were not far off. And probably in the distant ages of the great cold, when the wizard-artists displayed their pictures there must have been criticism, disagreement, approval, and excitement expressed —just as today.

Last of all Lemozi brought forth some pictures on stone, the sketch-blocks of upper palaeolithic man. At first as you look at such a slab you can make out nothing clear or significant. There is a maze of lines running all over the surface. Then slowly, quite gradually out of the labyrinth of strokes and lines, you begin to distinguish the curve of a back, then here a leg, a head, or a hoof, and suddenly you recognize some creature or other. In prehistoric times the beholder was not numbed and distracted by a thousand scratches and scrawls, for the stone was again and again covered with a coat of red ochre, so that a flat and smooth painting-surface was produced. On this, fresh engravings and pictures were laid. The pigment has, of course, long since vanished and only the inextricable puzzle of lines remains. And here is still another proof that prehistoric art-schools existed where artists were trained and in which they drew, painted, carved, and learned how to make sculpture. Art must have been taken seriously, for the artist bore a great responsibility and to his task of creation he must have dedicated himself with devotion.

The abundance of engravings and drawings was astonishing, and they came from a number of different sites at which Lemozi had dug over a long period of years. His excavations had cost him much time and money but the results fully justified all the trouble he had taken. And one of the most interesting things about these small art-objects was that they were all recovered from systematically and carefully worked-over strata. The pieces could be identified as belonging to the different culture-phases of the Magdalenian period of which, according to Breuil, no less than six are distinguishable although they do not necessarily, everywhere, form a chronological sequence.

Among Lemozi's treasures were also specimens of Aurignacian art—plain, but by no means "primitive," outlines. Then there were many examples of mid-Magdalenian art, freer in design, exceptionally dextrous in execution—without rigorously defined contours, but showing great fertility of inventiveness. The appearance of depth is skillfully conveyed and, as we have seen before, various technical problems, such as those relating to the representation of movement, of perspective in space, of front and rear views, are ingeniously solved. With the later phases of the Magdalenian we again find bold, delicately drawn, but very sure strokes. These constitute, then, another linear art which, however, is not wholly confined to outlines but, with immense virtuosity, sometimes dispenses with outlines altogether and gives us pictures closely resembling those executed in India ink by the Japanese masters of the school generally associated with the Zen sect of Buddhism.

A complete sequence of art-styles can be constituted with the aid of objects excavated from what we may call "self-dated" strata, which pieces in their turn enable us to establish what is at least a relative dating for the paintings and engravings to be seen upon the walls of grottoes and caves.

Lemozi and I had a long conversation about prehistoric sketches and trial-pieces. We compared notes on the occurrence of preliminary sketches and finished paintings at El Castillo, at Hornos de la Peña, and at Altamira. We decided that altogether the most striking example was that of the Font-de-Gaume, since a sketch for one of its paintings turned up at the Abri de la Genière (Ain department), a good hundred and eighty miles away from Les Eyzies, where the Font-de-Gaume grotto is situated.

We discussed these matters for a long time, and when at last we had to take leave of the Abbé Lemozi, and when Cabrerets lay far behind us, we felt that we had been favored that day with a really illuminating glimpse into the evolution of prehistoric cultures and into the development of the earliest arts upon this earth.

Sitting in the train and gazing out over the fields, the woods, the hills and the heights, we really felt rather proud to belong to the generation which has been able to look back so far. For before our times no one could see, with any degree of clarity and reliability, what happened in the earliest phases of man's artistic creation. We, today, are the first of our kind to be able to give an intelligible answer to the questions "How did art arise?" "What were its first stages?" "What were its earliest manifestations?"

You and I, and all of us, are singularly privileged in that we are able to utilize the material recovered by excavation, so that we no longer have to rely upon surmise, speculation, and guesswork, as did Goethe, Schiller, Herder, and the nineteenth-century aestheticians when they ventured to inquire into the origins of man's artistic creations.

We can view and examine specimens of the most ancient art. We can handle the art-objects fashioned thousands and thousands of years before the beginning of history. We can stand before upper palaeolithic paintings and study stroke by stroke the technique, the style, the tradition. We can, in fact, come to grips with one of the most puzzling problems in mankind's story, for we can as it were peer into our remote ancestors' studios and in a measure communicate with them in their act of creation.

VIII: Minateda

The music was entrancing. The great hotel hall was filled with people in evening dress. Couples dancing. Beautiful jewels. Many of the lovely ladies were wearing tiaras and had glittering diamonds in their hair. At the entrance we could see girls and women with mantillas, lace kerchiefs kept in place with large combs on the head.

"It's a prehistoric bit of clothing," said Professor Obermaier, whom I was sitting next to and with whom I had dined in the hotel, "it's a head-covering you meet with in Iberian sculpture of the fifth and fourth centuries B.C."

"It's wonderful how long some things—customs and traditions, for instance—do last . . . and costumes too. . . ."

"If you're in Madrid this Easter you will see all the smart Spanish women and girls wearing mantillas or veils. Even the Queen wears one. In fact, nearly everyone feels that this piece of apparel is most ancient and, therefore, highly respectable and not to be relinquished."

Just as he had finished saying this Frobenius entered the hall, noticed us, and came across to join us.

"Now all the old prehistoric rock-pictures are gathered together," he laughed. He was in excellent spirits, called the waiter and ordered drinks. Then we got deep into conversation.

We spoke of Breuil, of Paris, of rock-paintings in general, of the discoveries on Iberian sites, of the find of gold objects at Aliseda.

"The thing I'd most like to discover would be the age of the Levantine Spanish rock-pictures," I remarked.

"Well, if you ask my opinion I've no hesitation in saying

that I judge them to be of Old Stone Age, that is to say Ice Age, date."

To this statement of Obermaier's Frobenius added: "And I'd like to support that."

"But what worries me is the lack of proof; where is the proof for an Ice Age dating?"

"I'll admit," retorted Frobenius, "that this problem is one of the most complicated and baffling in all the range of prehistoric archaeology. Still, the three of us here in Madrid ought to be clever enough to solve the mystery."

"I'm afraid that doesn't look very likely," I had to put in. "We three are good friends, we work at the same subjects, we have published books devoted to similar themes, but on this one point of the Levantine Spanish art we're not of one mind, or let's say we're no longer of one mind."

"But in your big book on Ice Age art, the one you published in 1929, you also declared that the Levantine Spanish prehistoric pictures must be of glacial age," countered Obermaier as he turned toward me, raised his glass, and drank long and thoughtfully.

"But I just can't bring myself now to believe what I did in 1929. In fact, I've got to contradict myself. To confess the whole truth I must say that when I wrote what I did I was under your influence; and, moreover, Breuil completed my conversion, although I did hold out against him a long time, you know."

"Ah, yes, I can recall now," put in Frobenius; "in your earlier book, *The Art of Primitive Peoples*, you placed the Levantine Spanish art in mesolithic times, and then in your later book you changed over and attributed these same pictures to the palaeolithic, that is to say to Ice Age times."

"Yes, and that's all an illustration of how unreliable the evidence is and how patchy and scrappy our knowledge of the subject remains. Still, there the pictures are, they exist, and my feeling is that one must have it out with them, so to speak."

"Well, it's much the same with all discoveries, at least

archaeological ones. Things emerge from the earth, objects are found. Of course, they enrich our knowledge just because they exist, but we may have to wait a long time before we come to understand how to appraise and how to classify the evidence."

"I don't understand your misgivings at all," remarked Obermaier. "Anyway, for Breuil and me, it's always been crystal-clear that the Levantine rock-paintings belong to the Ice Age."

"But the style is quite different from the pictures of undoubted Ice Age art, those of the so-called Franco-Cantabrian group, in southwestern France and northern Spain. In these latter works the great mass of the pictures is composed of individual animals, of beasts seen in movement, often in a momentary flash of action. Perspective is employed, an appearance of depth in space is conveyed, and the problems are solved which relate to mass, or to hind or front views. In fact, we have a style which, in its naturalistic truthfulness, is much like that of the modern Impressionists."

"And in what way is the Levantine Spanish art essentially anything else?" asked Obermaier.

"Well, all I can say is that, for me, it is something quite different. The human figures, for instance, all highly stylized—that's something never found in Franco-Cantabrian prehistoric art. At a single glance one can always tell a Levantine picture from one of the Franco-Cantabrian complex."

"But in the Levantine rock-paintings, animals are often depicted in a quite realistic manner."

"Still, they are different and most decidedly different from the beasts in Franco-Cantabrian art. Moreover, in the Levantine sites there are, practically speaking, no polychrome paintings. Everything is like a shadow-show image seen upon a screen and, above all, represented all on one plane. In fact, that's what is, for me, the main difference in style and tradition between the Levantine pictures and those of farther north. In the Franco-Cantabrian group you've got an appearance of depth, whereas in Levantine Spanish art there is no appearance of depth, of perspective, at all."

The music died down. The couples separated and made their way back to their places. Lively chatter, laughter, and the tinkle of glasses. Still, we hardly noticed when the orchestra struck up once more. Anyway, the music seemed to come echoing from a distance.

I started off again. "And you know, I can't help thinking that there's some significance in what happened during later, much later, phases of art history. The transition from naturalism to stylization crops up again and again. Something like confirmation of my view is afforded, it seems to me, by the constantly recurring transformations in the history of art. Even in our own time we had Expressionism following Impressionism, while after the Classical came the post-Classical with its stressing of plane surfaces. After the Cretan art of the sixteenth century B.C. we get the very stylized art of Mycenae in the fourteenth century B.C. with its flat and plane surfaces. And this latter, we may remember, followed on after an art-period during which men were much preoccupied with the problem of the representation of depth, in fact with the endeavor to portray three dimensions while utilizing only two. Judging, then, from these known examples in art history I'm inclined to think that the Spanish Levantine pictures, with their accent on plane surfaces and on outlines, belong to a later art than that of the Franco-Cantabrian group."

"But, following your argument, after stylization we always get an abstract art," countered Obermaier, "and this entirely abstract art we find, of course, in Azilian times and with the stylized human figures upon the polychrome pebbles recovered from Mas d'Azil and other mesolithic sites. Therefore, it seems to me that the Levantine Spanish art, which is much more naturalistic than anything of Azilian or, indeed, mesolithic dating, must come well before the

Azilian even if the Levantine does appear, at times, a little stylized."

"There's an objection to that argument, and I think it's a weighty one. Possibly those stylized Azilian figures you mention are symbolical signs—talismans, maybe, or something of the like. Possibly such things were not the main artistic manifestations of their epoch. It is even possible that such stylized art was merely local and that its representative objects do not indicate any decisive general modification of art tradition or style."

Upon this, Frobenius turned to Obermaier and asked: "As a matter of fact, perhaps you might let us know what you consider to be the most weighty arguments in favor of an Ice Age dating for the Levantine Spanish art."

As may be imagined, I listened very carefully indeed to Obermaier's reply.

"In my opinion the most decisive indication of great antiquity lies in their content; in what they depict. They disclose to us a world of hunters. Nowhere is there any hint at any sort of agriculture. There are no representations of carts, plows, or hatchets, such as for instance occur in the Swedish rock-pictures. Moreover, there are no cattle harnessed to vehicles, such as are found in the Italian pictoglyphs. The world of the Levantine Spanish artists is a world of hunters and food-gatherers, in fact a society typical of Ice Age times. The pictures are of men with bows and arrows, of hunters who follow the tracks of beasts, there are representations of battues, of animals dead and dying—all showing, as I have said, a hunters' and not an agriculturalists' world."

"But we never come across any picture of a cold-loving animal," I objected. "Where are the figures of bisons, rhinoceroses, mammoths, or reindeer? Even the elk mentioned by Breuil—and copied by him—is by no means certainly an elk. The thing occurs on a rock-painting at Alpera in the province of Albacete. Several times I've isolated this drawing and have studied it carefully, but my opinion is that no certain conclusion can be drawn from this figure. Maybe it's not an elk at all; the apparently broad muzzle may be due to the fact that there is another picture underneath the 'elk' figure, though the lower painting is not at present distinguishable. I should say that the whole of the Levantine fauna indicates clearly a post-glacial age for the paintings of eastern Spain."

"But even during the Ice Age there were hardly any cold-loving animals in Spain," retorted Obermaier. "Bones of reindeer, for instance, are quite rare."

"Still, they do exist all the same, and since not a single reindeer occurs in the Levantine pictures, I should say that's an indication of post-glacial age. Mind you, it's not been easy for me to relinquish the theory that these pictures are of Ice Age date, especially as I've written a lot about them as of such period, and no one likes very much to recant and to deny what he has championed."

"The way I look at it is this," went on Obermaier. "We've got to imagine two peoples who lived contemporaneously in Ice Age times. First of all there's a northern group of peoples with Aurignacian, Solutrean, and Magdalenian cultures. These are the tribes who created the Franco-Cantabrian Ice Age art. And we are quite sure of the dating of this art, since in stratified cave-fillings have been found small objects corresponding to the larger paintings upon the walls. Now, as I see it, at the same epoch as these northern tribes, there flourished, to the south of the Pyrenean-Cantabrian mountain-chain, and especially in eastern Spain, another people or group of peoples. These, therefore, were also Ice Age folk and their characteristic cultures are early, middle, and late Capsian. That's my view in a nutshell."

"And that used to be the way I saw things too, but I was forced to change my opinion. In no known site can it be proved that Capsian-culture objects are of Ice Age date; in fact, quite on the contrary, the Capsian layers always occur above Ice Age deposits, while in North Africa, Capsian artifacts are found associated with pottery fragments—as Vaufrey has conclusively demonstrated. I think that your theory would hold water only if we had to deal with two culture-areas completely isolated the one from the other— in other words, if there had been an impassable barrier separating the Franco-Cantabrian area from the Levantine Spanish region. But this is not the case. There are plenty of 'Franco-Cantabrian' sites scattered over central and even southern Spain. For instance, there's the Parpalló cave near Gandía where no less than sixty small art-objects have been discovered. They are all in the Franco-Cantabrian mid-Magdalenian tradition and style. It is, then, obvious just from this Parpalló evidence alone that it's impossible to maintain the hypothesis that there were two Ice Age culture-areas, mutually exclusive."

"Yes, I see your point," admitted Obermaier, "and perhaps we must probe still deeper into the problem of the age of the Levantine pictures. It's always possible we've made a mistake, that's never impossible, especially in the case of quite new discoveries. And you know I'm the last man in the world to stick to a thing that I've declared once, just because I've said it."

He took up his glass and drank again. Then, quite suddenly, he stared at me and said:

"Now, get off and visit the most important of all Ice Age art-sites—Minateda."

"That's a very good idea, but how long does it take to get to Minateda and where is it?"

"If you leave early in the afternoon you can travel all night and be there the next morning. Minateda isn't so very far from Cartagena, though it's not right on the coast, all the same; and I must tell you that there's no village or hamlet of Minateda, there are just three or four houses, and you'll have to spend the night in the cottage of the pointsman who looks after the station."

I lost no time; the very next day I was in the train bound for Minateda. My compartment was crammed full with peasants in their local costumes, and a few commercial travelers. Their conversation turned on bad markets and falling prices.

Madrid was only a few miles behind when the stony desolation of the landscape seemed to spread to infinity. No signs of life. Very few trees, even. Railroad tracks, slopes, houses clinging to slopes, and all around nothing but stone and rock, nothing living, no signs of living things. Typically Spanish.

My traveling-companions began to unpack their hampers. Tortillas, roast chicken, and red wine in wrapped-up bottles. It was all offered to me, and despite my protests I was forced to take a nibble at everything. The whole compartment was interested. I was the subject of uninterrupted conversation, but no one ventured to address a question directly to me.

After some time, however, one of the men plucked up his courage and asked if I were French. "No," I answered, "I'm a German." Then they all looked at me and one said that Germany was a large country. "It's got nearly twice as many inhabitants as France," he explained. Another man asked me if it was not very cold in Germany, so cold, in fact, that people froze to death there. And everybody expressed astonishment at the long journey I had made from Germany all the way to Spain. South America, even, seemed nearer to them than Germany, for Spanish is spoken in South America, whereas Germany—well, that was a very long way away indeed. Conversation now switched to politics and foreign policies. France, for instance, well, that was pretty dangerous, it was too near—but Germany, well, that was a long way off, and there would never be war between Spain and Germany. Besides, Germany was very big and rich and there must be a lot of large cities there. Spain ought to have an alliance with Germany, one opined. Thereupon, a little fellow sitting in one of the corner seats took up the conversation and explained that Charles the Fifth had been a German and his reign had been the most prosperous period Spain had ever known. Everyone in the compartment looked with respect at such a historical scholar, and in order to sustain his role he took a book from his pocket and began to read.

Slowly darkness crept over the land and everyone settled down for the night. They all took their shoes off, tucked their clothes over themselves, ate a few last oranges, stretched out their feet to the opposite seats. Before long nothing could be heard but a strident cacophony of snores. I stared out of the window. One could make out the same stony scenery. A few lights gliding here and there; but, for the rest, stone and still more stone. About six o'clock in the morning the train came to a stop at the Minateda way-side station. I got out and except for the pointsman's cottage could see no other dwelling at all amid a chaos of stones and boulders and rocky cliffs. I went up to the pointsman and told him I wanted to see the paintings. He pointed right up to the top of the mountains and said:

"That's where they are, right up there, in a sort of fold of the rocks, that's where they are."

"But how can I get there?"

"Get there? Well, there's no donkey if that's what you're thinking of . . . but my daughter could go with you if you like." And he introduced me to his daughter.

Then I asked where I could spend the night but no, there was absolutely no possibility of that . . . there was only one arrangement, his daughter would have to give up her room to me; that was to say, her corner of the guard-house. She could bed down on the floor. That would be all right for two or three nights. Anyway, the pointsman was nice and friendly. He produced a basket with wine and omelette and the daughter and I set off. She was twelve years old, very lively and active, with very dark eyes and black hair parted down the middle. Her legs were very brown and she jumped with her naked feet from one stone to another. She told me that two or three years before another German had come to study the rock-paintings—so, naturally, when we met a man riding upon a donkey she called out to him that yet another German had arrived to look at the pictures.

After some time we got to a small olive-grove, and though even here the ground was sterile-looking and bare there was a little soil to be seen. But the stones soon prevailed once more. Hopping from one stone to another one had to be careful not to twist an ankle; the going was so toilsome that from time to time I had to take a rest and gaze along the road we had come.

Stone, nothing but stone, and beyond, the little olive-grove, and then the three or four gray dwellings of Minateda.

Barranco de la Mortaja, the "Ravine of the Shroud," or it might be "of the Mortise," is the name given to the mountain gorge where the prehistoric pictures of Minateda are. The nearer I got to the site the more clearly it seemed to me that it consisted essentially of a long, overhanging shelf of rock-formation. When we finally got up to the recess in the cliff-face we dumped our basket, drawing-paper and camera on the ground and then I set off to examine the layout and disposition of the painted walls. The rock-shelter opens eastward and the roof projects over the rock-face for a distance ranging from about three to approximately six feet. At the foot and in the front of the recess thus formed, a sort of platform widens out. It is, of course, the rear wall of the recess that bears the pictures. I paced their whole length and measured my steps. I reckoned that there were no less than twenty-one yards of paintings. In many places the frieze is fully seven feet broad, though toward the edges the figures are noticeably fewer in number than toward the center. The whole recess is some twenty-eight yards broad, and in places the rear wall is as much as eight yards in from the platform. One has only to take a casual glance at the pictures to be convinced that they represented many different periods. The uppermost layers—presumably the most recent pictures—

are the most stylized and also the brightest in color. The figures form an astonishing maze or medley of forms, cutting into one another and overlying one another, but one can distinguish clearly enough that the more stylized figures are on the top of those in naturalistic tradition. There has been repeated overpainting, and this is highly significant.

My first thoughts were that, at last, I was really getting somewhere in my search for the solution of the problem presented by the dating of the Spanish Levantine pictures. Yes, Obermaier had been quite right in recommending that I visit the Minateda ravine. It seems to me that this is the largest of all the Levantine friezes yet discovered.

The most recent assemblage of paintings is, then, relatively easy to recognize; and the most ancient figures are also not very difficult to pick out. They are large-scale representations of animals together with some human figures, though these are hardly depicted with the same naturalness and movement as the beasts are. I am of the opinion that these Minateda animal-figures are certainly of Ice Age date, although they show no attempt at indication of depth or perspective. At least, such endeavors to indicate perspective as there are make a very feeble impression—as, for instance, in the case of a large bovine, an ox, on the left-hand side of the frieze. The animals depicted are reindeer, stags, horses, and ibexes—and at least two rhinoceroses can be seen . . . or can they? I thought to myself, "Well, here we are, rhinoceroses, clear proof of the glacial age of the paintings; or did these beasts survive hereabouts until later times?" . . . but the longer I gazed at the rhinoceros picture the more convinced I became that it was not at all clear or certain. The two horns might belong to a painting underneath, a picture that was part of some other animal . . . and then the legs looked far too long for those of a rhinoceros. So it seemed as though arguments based on rhinoceros figures at Minateda must be inconclusive, since the pictures themselves are so confused. My own impression is that nothing at Minateda is undoubtedly of Ice Age date; and, in fact, the more I examined the frieze the more convinced I became that everything I saw presented characteristics so unlike those of any Old Stone Age art that Minateda cannot possibly be assigned to Ice Age artists. The mass of human figures in all sorts of lively attitudes—jumping, scurrying, running—the very pronounced stylization of the essential, determining features of the figures . . . all very different in spirit and in execution from any undoubtedly Ice Age art.

Indeed, what we see at Minateda is a completely different style altogether. We are beholding two different worlds when we look at, say, a fresco at Altamira or Lascaux and then examine the paintings of Minateda. The Ice Age world is something wholly real, wholly factual, firmly rooted and anchored in the present. The world of the Minateda rock-paintings is one of man's imagination. It is subjective. Even in its essence, it is abstract. All the forms are modified, compressed, or changed at the imperative command of an overriding idea. In fact some "idea," and not a desire to imitate life, is the determining factor in the Minateda art. An abstract art, however, must surely come later than a "concrete" one, for the abstract is the continuation, into the realm of imagination and fantasy, of something actually experienced in the world of fact. The abstract is a subjective conquest of reality. The abstract reflects some unifying concept, some general idea which may, of course, be represented in all the details, but which can only be fully realized when all those details have been thoroughly "absorbed," so to speak. As far as we can see, the abstract always comes later than the concrete. Anything we can call "abstract thought" comes after the perception of isolated, or at least individual, things or phenomena. So, in my opinion anyway, a stylized art must be later than a naturalistic one. I cannot hold to be true what is so often stated, namely that the abstract is "primitive," and characteristic of early man.

I moved from picture to picture. There are hundreds on

the rock-face, and I paid especial attention to the over-painting. In one spot, for instance, there is a stylized, masculine figure, quite upright—it is painted over the picture of some animal. Then you can recognize, in other parts of the frieze, women wearing long, cloche-shaped skirts, and they, too, were executed over some now almost obliterated animal-figures. There are so many layers, indeed, that the many different overpaintings are not all easy to distinguish one from another. Sometimes, for instance, a human form cuts only into the edge of an animal underneath. Very often, nevertheless, the figure of a man or a woman is set

Paintings in red. One-half actual size. Minateda, near Hellín, Spain.

right across an earlier animal-form, just as though the artist had paid no attention at all to the animals he was marring and covering.

Nothing at Minateda puzzled me more than this persistent overpainting; there are so very many layers to be distinguished. Yet to the right and to the left of the frieze there is plenty of unutilized space on the rock-face; still the artists painted repeatedly on the same spots of the surface. Obviously, these particular spots must have been ones which brought signal good luck—for, of course, pictures are intimately bound up with ritual and cult; and this was true not only in Ice Age times, but also in the later mesolithic, neolithic, and Bronze Age periods and, indeed, in the Middle Ages. It is, to some extent anyway, true of our own days.

If one looks around one at Minateda it is not difficult to realize how the site came to have a sacred significance. The whole scene seems specially created for rites and ceremonies: the impressive overhanging rock, the fine recess, often in the shadow but, still again, often wholly exposed to the light of day; the wide-reaching view over the valley, the platform before the recess, a platform upon which a considerable concourse of people might gather. . . . Certainly, I thought, there must be, hereabouts, other rock-recesses in which pictures exist. So I got up and walked over, first to the right-hand side and then to the left-hand side of the great recess. I told the pointsman's daughter that she might stay where she was, but she faithfully followed me. So, together, we made our way along the whole side of the ridge. Quite suddenly I discovered another recess with a lot more paintings, stylized, even strongly schematic, masculine figures resolving themselves into arcs, triangles and circles. These figures almost certainly date from Bronze Age times, for in Bronze Age deposits (that is to say, containing copper daggers and arrowheads together with pottery vessels), a great quantity of cult-idols has been recovered, and these latter are of identical form and arrangement with the figures portrayed on this Minateda recess. Another proof, if one were needed, that stylization is a later phenomenon than naturalistic portrayal. The art of the Bronze Age, for instance, is fully stylized. The Peña Tu prehistoric painted rock, not very far from Barcelona, affords an interesting example of dating. Near the painted idol (of a form quite similar to that occurring in Bronze Age deposits) is represented a dagger with three nails. And such daggers are found only in Period I of the Bronze Age. In Spain that lasted from about 2000 to 1800 B.C. Thus we can date the Peña Tu frescoes to within a couple of centuries.

The Minateda paintings are still almost unknown but then, after all, that is hardly surprising since the whole assemblage of Levantine Spanish prehistoric art is very little known. In 1920 Breuil published a short report on Minateda, but no monograph on the rock-pictures has yet been written, though such a volume would be of the utmost value. There are hundreds of figures preserved at Minateda, and in no other site that I know of are the various layers of painting and overpainting so clearly distinguishable as here.

When we got back to the main recess, we noticed that about twenty men had turned up and were apparently waiting for us. They were chattering excitely about the *tesoro*, the "treasure" the German had come to find. They were in no sort of doubt that the pictures were clear pointers indicating the presence of buried treasure. Every motion of my hand was carefully watched, how I drew, what I photographed and measured. Not one of the crowd lost sight of me for an instant.*

And now I began to understand why the pointsman's daughter was so faithful in following me about everywhere.

The closer I examined the frescoes the clearer I began to see into the problem of dating. Everywhere the more stylized paintings were the more recent, for everywhere they overlay the realistic, or naturalistic, figures; though none of these, in my opinion, is as naturalistic as we find in Ice Age paintings. In fact, the longer I scrutinized and studied, the more convinced I became that Spanish Levantine art—let's say as represented at Minateda, anyway— must not be attributed to an Ice Age dating. Breuil and

* In justice to the local inhabitants it must not be forgotten that, in recent years, not a few "treasures" of gold objects have been found in Spain. (*Translator's note.*)

Obermaier were surely mistaken, and I must revise my earlier estimates. If only there were anything to excavate at the foot of Minateda Rock!

As a matter of fact, I did dig in the Valltorta Gorge and there discovered late Capsian-type artifacts, microliths most certainly attributable to post-glacial times.

But, at Minateda, although I carefully went over the whole space at the base of the rock-face, I found nothing but bed-rock. Then I went off to the right, and then again to the left, and all my visitors followed—not for one second did they leave me alone. Then, there, the supreme moment arrived. In one spot I did begin to ply my spade. It was where there was a little earth and soil. Faces took on a still more intent expression. Eyes were sparkling, gestures got more and more lively. Everyone was talking at once and commenting on every phase of the proceedings. Again and again one word and one word only struck upon my ear: *tesoro, tesoro*. It was not very long before I had a few stones in my hand, worked stones, implements. As I brushed them clean with my fingers I could see that here, as in the Valltorta Gorge, I had come across microliths, small chipped arrowheads, tiny trapeziums, small semi-circular segments, delicate little knives of very careful workmanship. But nothing of all this was palaeolithic, that is to say of Ice Age date, for in Old Stone Age times such microliths as these were unknown. I dug down a bit deeper. The eyes around me got ever tenser and tenser. But I struck no Ice Age stratum. So my summary excavation at Minateda indicated an epoch comparable to that revealed at the Valltorta Gorge: one characterized by implements solely of post-glacial age.

It is, of course, true enough that the exact age of the Minateda or Valltorta paintings is not determined by such finds of microlithic culture-objects. Still, I am convinced that the style, the technique, and the subjectivism or Expressionism in the attitude of the figures indicate clearly a mesolithic and early neolithic dating for an art of transition, between the naturalism of the Ice Age on the one hand and the complete stylization of the Bronze Age on the other hand. Such a view simplifies and clarifies the picture of man's artistic and cultural development. So we have three main art-styles: the Impressionistic in the Ice Age, the Expressionistic in the mesolithic Levantine Spanish rock-paintings and, then, the wholly stylized, Cubist forms of the Bronze Age and later.

By midday the sun was mighty hot. My little guide and I sat down in the shade of the overhanging rock-shelf and ate our omelette while all around us the men stood and stared. There was, of course, a lively conversation going on but I could not catch it all. The Spanish was too fast for me, and the local dialect is by no means easy to follow anyway. But I did make out enough to discover that the general feeling was one of cheerfulness, even optimism. The German, that was true, had not yet found the *tesoro*, but he was obviously a widely traveled man, he had taken a great deal of trouble, he was certainly a clever and learned person who could read the inscriptions of Goth and Moor—and yet, all the same, he had not been able to light upon the *tesoro*.

It became quite clear that two distinct and, indeed, opposing groups had been formed. There were those who still thought I was going to find the *tesoro*, and those who had given up all hope. But not a single man of either group was going to let me out of his sight for one instant. As I shoveled the earth back into the little hole I had made, I noticed that they all appeared very disappointed. But their interest perked up again and they became very keen when they saw I was beginning to draw. I would put the sheet of paper near the figure I was going to copy—obviously an indication that the *Alemán* could decipher the inscription. Somewhere or other on the surface of the frieze it must be written where the *tesoro* was hidden—otherwise, naturally, all the pictures and figures would have no sense. Then would the *Alemán* have come all the way to Minateda if he did not know how to read the riddle?

Finally an elderly peasant came up to me. He had an interesting face, baked brown by the sun. His features stood out sharp and his dark eyes lent him a sage and wise appearance. One could see that he was the descendant of a noble race. His striking visage reflected an immemorial past.

"If you don't find the treasure now," he asked, "will you go right back to Germany?"

"Oh, but I'm not looking for treasure, I just want to study these rock-paintings. They're thousands of years old, important documents for the history of mankind, for the story of man's art."

But he only laughed. Obviously he did not believe one word I said. Soon they were all laughing. So the only thing I could do was to go on quietly working. Quite clearly nothing I could say would convince them that I was not looking for *tesoro*.

"There was a gentleman here once," went on the same peasant, "he came from France"—clearly he was referring to Breuil—"but he did not find the *tesoro*. Now you've come but I don't think you're going to discover it either. But someone will find it one day and then Minateda will be big and rich."

I worked on steadily through the whole afternoon and until the evening. Still the men stayed around me. When the sun had set I packed up the drawing things in the basket, and then my little guide and I made our way off down the mountainside.

During the night I could hardly sleep in my bunk. I kept on thinking about the age of the rock-paintings, about the overpainting, about the succession of layers—and, strangely enough, such is the power of suggestion, through all my dreams I was haunted by an eerie belief in the famous *tesoro*.

The next day, while I was working at copying the frescoes, I found that I had even more visitors than on the first occasion. . . . On the third day I took the train back to Madrid.

By the evening I was again sitting by Obermaier's side in the hotel.

"I was immensely impressed by Minateda, and I think I can now see a bit more clearly into the problem of the Levantine pictures' age. I cannot agree that they are of Ice Age date. There are no pictures of Ice Age fauna, and the style and technique of the drawing is quite different from what we are familiar with in pictures of undoubted Old Stone Age dating. The pronounced stylization—especially noticeable in the human figures—and the tendency to Expressionism lends the whole Minateda complex a quite different tone and 'atmosphere' from those of the Franco-Cantabrian pictures. One can notice the transitions in the different layers of the paintings. The oldest pictures at Minateda may possibly date back to Ice Age times. They have something of the quality of the Franco-Cantabrian late palaeolithic art. But the later Minateda pictures, superposed upon the bottom layers, show a progressively marked stylization, so that the latest figures of all, those which lie on the top, are so thoroughly stylized as to be in many cases almost or quite Cubist."

"I'm still not fully convinced," replied Obermaier. "I must discuss the whole matter with Breuil once more and, then, I'll have to go myself to Minateda again. You knew, of course, that the Spaniards in general, and in particular Cabre Aguiló and Hernandez Pacheco, never believed in our theory of the Ice Age date for the pictures of Levantine Spain? So there have always been archaeologists who have stood out for a comparatively recent dating. Now if you join up with them, well, I must say that our hypothesis will be rather shaken. Yes, we'll have to go into the whole matter again and undertake a full-scale investigation."

"Now after this visit to Minateda I'm quite clear in my own mind, for I don't think there's any site in Levantine

Portion of the Great Frieze. One-tenth actual s[...]

m a copy by H. Breuil. Minateda, near Hellín, Spain.

Spain where I could better see the stages of evolution than at Minateda. An examination of the frieze there is enough to furnish one with a complete view of the development of art-styles in prehistoric times. Then, for instance, at Las Canforras and at the Gasulla Ravine there are pictures of men leading animals by halters. Such paintings as these cannot possibly belong to Ice Age times. My conclusion is that the whole of the Spanish Levantine group is of post-glacial date, in fact, that the frescoes begin just after the Ice Age epoch and run on right into neolithic times."

"You may be right," answered Obermaier; "in any scientific discipline better knowledge drives out good. We must ever seek to know more and more thoroughly, and there will always be problems which cannot be wholly solved."

"Well, all the same, Minateda was a wonderful experience." And I raised my glass to Obermaier. "I can't thank you enough for having urged me to go there. I saw much and I learned much. In these last three days I've been able to see far back in time, into stages of art and religion which were unfamiliar to me and which were hidden from all of us until a short while ago."

IX: Valltorta

The motor-bus was rattling and jangling along a road which was winding and forever rising. Far behind us we could see the coast, the broad blue sea, and the red roofs of Castellón de la Plana. That way, up there, lies Barcelona, while in the other direction, toward the south, is Valencia.

It was a magnificent day, the sky bright blue with a few white wispy clouds floating in the air. The bus was filled with Spanish country people, peasants and their women-folk. In front of me sat a buxom woman with two small children in her arms. She asked us where we were going and we answered, "Albocácer."

"Have you got relations there?"

"No, not at all, we're Germans and we don't know any-one in this part of the world."

All the people in the bus were listening and they heard this declaration with astonishment.

"So you've got business there, I suppose," went on the woman.

"No, we want to study rock-pictures that exist in the neighborhood of Albocácer."

"Oh, I know what you mean, they're signs and marks made by the Moors. They had a lot of gold, you know, and that's where they buried it."

I tried to explain to her that the pictures were much older than the Moors but she would not believe me. A white-haired man in the corner of the bus began to examine us rather sharply. Then, as one of her babies cried, the woman slowly undid her blouse, pulled out her left breast and offered it to the infant; whereupon the other baby started whimpering, so she gave it her other breast. The

twins thereupon made no more noise but that of the suck-
ing of their mother's milk. Presently she removed both
babies, reached down under the seat, pulled up two little
gray puppies and suckled them. While the puppies were
drinking the babies fondled them. A curious sight for us,
puppies being suckled by a woman, but no one in the bus
seemed to be the slightest bit astonished.

"The puppies were thirsty, too," explained the woman
as, quite slowly, she let her breasts slip back into her blouse
and then buttoned it up.

By now, to our right and to our left, instead of orange
groves, were clumps of olives, and then these got fewer
and fewer. We were approaching the world of the great
Spanish tableland: rocks, stones, boulders, bare heights,
gorges, vales, cliffs, and a few isolated olive trees.

In a couple of hours we got to Albocácer. The inn was
of the sort usual in Spanish villages but the innkeeper's wife
had fair hair and one might have taken her for a North
European woman. She led us to our room and, as we were
unpacking, a policeman appeared.

"You are a spy, sir; you've got a map of the region, and
I've got orders to arrest you."

"A spy? What do you mean? Here are our passports."

"Oh, yes, but the passports are made out in French and
no one hereabouts can read French, not even the mayor and
he's a most clever and well-educated man."

"But they're not in French, they're in German."

"You mean to say you're not French?"

"No, indeed we're not, we're Germans."

"Oh, well, of course in that case it may well be that
you're not spies. By the way, whereabouts is Germany?"

"Germany? Well, I'll tell you. Germany's a long way
away from here, in fact it's so far away that it's too far for
spies; they can't get from Germany all the way to Spain."

For a moment he seemed satisfied, then his face hardened
again. "But if you're not spies what have you come here for
and why have you got a map?"

"We've come here to study prehistoric rock-paintings. I'm a professor at Cologne University."

"Then, of course, you know Don Hugo?"

"Why, of course I know him, know him very well indeed, just look at this"—and I pulled out Hugo Obermaier's book on the Valltorta Ravine and showed it to him, together with the map in the volume.

Again and again he read the line where the word "Albocácer" occurred. Very, very slowly he spelled it out, letter by letter: A L B O C Á C E R.

"So people in Germany, too, have heard of Albocácer? And of the Barranco de Valltorta? And you've come all the way from Germany just to see the pictures on the rocks?"

"Just that, and Albocácer's a famous place"—the man's eyes lighted up—"and it became famous through Don Hugo."

"Ah, Don Hugo, there's a charming man for you. And so learned too. He's a professor at Madrid University, but he's not a bit stand-offish, he's friendly with everyone, he's got a nice word for everyone he meets, and once he gave me some cigarettes."

Thinking this might be a hint, I pulled out my case. I could not very well lag behind Don Hugo. This timely gesture set the seal upon my friendship with the policeman. With considerable difficulty he puzzled out the author's name on the book: Hugo Obermaier, *Catedrático de la Universidad de Madrid*, but the German surname was a hard stumbling-block.

"Of course you know Don Hugo's German too?" With these words I managed to dispel all the remaining suspicions lingering in the man's mind.

"But he's a professor at Madrid University all the same and he speaks Spanish like a Castilian and he lives in Madrid."

"Yes, he's a very celebrated man. He was a professor at Vienna University and then at Paris before moving to Madrid where his home now is. But, for all that you say, he learned his Spanish when he was already grown-up."

Then the policeman went on to tell us a lot about Don Hugo Obermaier, whose visits to Albocácer had been the great events in village history. Finally, the good fellow, after the usual Spanish compliments, took leave of us.

We went out for a stroll through the little town. The sun was sinking and the shadows lengthening. Off from the fields came the acrid odor of newly turned earth. Peasants were making their way homeward from the day's toil. The summits of the hills flamed in rose-red radiance.

When we got back to the house we could hear a cow lowing underneath our bedroom and then, soon, we began to discern the scent of baked meats. The kitchen stove was in the dining-room, or let us say dining-room and kitchen were one. In the oven we could see a chicken. It had not been drawn, but just plucked and then laid upon the hot embers. As we entered the room our hostess was turning the bird over and sprinkling it with salt. Then she waited a few minutes and pulled the chicken out from amid the glowing wood. She poured some more salt on the meat, placed it upon a dish and brought it to where we were sitting.

"*Pollo asado*," she said. "*Buen apetito.*"

We began our meal, but by our standards and to our taste the chicken's flesh was raw while its skin was burned to a cinder. All the time the door kept swinging back and forth as more and more people came in. Soon the dining-room-kitchen was crammed full. Everyone wanted to see the *Alemánes*. No one spoke a single word. Meanwhile we ate steadily into the raw chicken, but finally we had to give up. We could stand it no more. We took the chicken back to the lady of the house. She seemed inexpressibly shocked by our strange tastes and our odd manners but, after due reflection, she fried us some eggs. As we began to eat again one of the peasants asked for news of Don Hugo in Madrid. Another man opined that the rock-paintings

had been executed by the Visigoths since hereabouts there
had been, in olden times, much fighting between them and
the Moors. In fact, there were demons and evil spirits
which still lingered about the sites. It was especially dangerous to approach the pictures since they might come to
life and kill any onlookers.

A third peasant confirmed these opinions and added that
not a few people had already been brought to destruction
by the malevolence of the spirits. For instance there was a
shepherd who had died in the preceding year. It was quite
certain that he had not just suffered a fall. He had been
slain by the *demonios*. After that, they all began speaking
at once and giving us good advice. We must not forget to
make an *higo* or "fig" with our right hands; that is, push
up our thumbs between our index and middle fingers . . .
and keep them like that . . . that was the gesture which
was sovereign against the power of the spirits . . . and
also very helpful against the baleful magic of the Evil Eye.

Then a little fellow came forward and told us that he did
not believe a word of all that. The rock-pictures were
without any doubt made by the Arabs when they hid their
treasures there. And in a moment the word *tesoro* was on
everyone's lips.

We went on eating but the differences of opinion soon
began to look serious. The company split into two opposing factions, one insisting on demons and the other on
treasure. Gestures and gesticulations got more and more
animated, and we rather lost the thread of the discussion.
Faces looked very tense and dark eyes sparkled with excitement. Then one of the men came forward and asked me
what my opinion was. I was a little nonplused, but then
had a brilliant idea. I ordered *cerveza*, beer, for everyone.
Soon a blessed calm descended upon the assembly and this
gave me an opportunity to inquire about a guide for the
next day. One man was bold enough to propose his services.
All the rest stared at him in a quizzical and somewhat dis-

concerted manner. He was actually going to defy the devils! But he laughed and when we had agreed upon a price and upon the time he left the room.

The next morning we were awakened by a cock crowing in the room next to ours; when we had heard a second and then a third, when the cow beneath us had commenced her lowing, then we were wide awake and, of course, covered with flea-bites. It was six o'clock and at seven the guide arrived carrying a basket packed with bread and milk. It was several hours' walk to the pictures. We crossed dried-up watercourses and brooks, we trudged through scrub and bushes, we plodded across fields, but it was a wonderful day. An immaculate blue vault of sky spanned the heavens far above us. The sun blazed down while birds twittered and wildflowers decked our path. On the hill slopes herds of cows were grazing.

After a good four hours of tramping, at about eleven o'clock we drew near to the Valltorta Ravine. There is a wide glen whose banks fall steeply down to a stream. Bushes and scrub cover the sides from top to bottom but cannot hide the large stones and boulders. If one chanced to step upon or against a stone it went tumbling, rumbling, down into the brook below. The ravine twisted and turned. Sometimes it was a quite narrow canyon and then again the gorge would widen out somewhat. The cliffs contain a number of natural recesses, little rock-shelters, from three to six feet deep. Many of them present no pictures, but then again others are crowded with paintings and drawings.

The first pictures we saw were in a recess called the Cueva del Civil; these look dark red against the yellowish background of the stone. Curiously enough, the flat places which would at first sight appear to offer the best surfaces for painting are hardly used at all, while the rough ones which seem unsuitable for drawing are covered with pictures. The pigment has sunk deep into the substance of the rock, and in various places it can be observed that the color has combined with the background to a depth of several millimeters. Such a phenomenon is of itself alone enough to prove that the pigment was applied millennia ago. We ran our fingers over some of the colored surfaces; they felt quite smooth and there was no trace of any difference in level between the painted and the unpainted places on the rock-face. It was clear that the color employed was ochre mixed with animal fat; in fact, oil pigment like that we use today.

The sun blazed down upon us. The view from the site was far-reaching over both valley and heights. This was the spot where prehistoric men sat, drew, painted, hunted. It was difficult to realize that thousands of years had elapsed between them and us. Difficult, because here was none of the mysterious magic of the subterranean grottoes, no damp walls, no murk, no glittering antechambers or throne-rooms of gorgeous stalactite. No, here everything was near to us. It was like yesterday—like magic in broad daylight, wizardry in the sunshine. . . .

The elongated human figures, men with bows and arrows, men hurrying, running, leaping. Many of the pictures are no larger than a man's hand. Others can easily be covered with two outstretched palms. In their foreshortening, their simplification, their stylization, these pictures are unquestionably Expressionist in execution. Some lie one above the other, or some partially cut into others. Then, many stand quite alone, isolated. The whole recess is a mass of paintings, a mass of men in movement, with a few stags.

We took some photographs, made some drawings, and then clambered along a pathless track which led through bushes and shrubs that ripped our clothes, scratched our legs. We were on our way to the other painted niches in the rocks. The first one we came to had no pictures, nor had the one after that, but before long we reached a recess with a most remarkable painting. A sort of fabulous beast, a wild boar with a bull's tail. Arrows were directed toward this monster. Our guide had a name for this site: the Cueva del Mas d'en Josep. This was quite obviously another magic

Levantine Spanish rock-paintings. (1) and (2) and (3): Valltorta Ravine, Province of Castellón de la Plana, Spain. (4) Alpera, Province of Albacete, Spain. (5) Cueva de Secans, Teruel, Spain.

picture and one, moreover, which had been modified in prehistoric times. An original portrayal, that of a bull, had no doubt been signally useful in attracting good luck, therefore the painting was worked over again and again. The arrows, alone, are a certain sign of sorcery.

I pulled Obermaier's book out of my pocket and looked

through it to find the picture; but it was not there. In fact, there was no mention in the volume of the Cueva del Mas d'en Josep at all. Then I remembered what Obermaier had told me in Madrid—that his book dealt with not more than half the Levantine pictures and that Bosch-Gimpera of Barcelona was to publish the rest. Only a small proportion of these had, however, actually been described or reproduced in a publication. So I thought to myself, "Here's an unworked field. I must look for—and, of course, discover—hitherto unknown prehistoric pictures."

We walked on, uphill and then downhill, peering into one recess and then into another. The stones kept rolling down into the stream and the loose scrub and brushwood afforded only a very insecure foothold. However, we had got onto a sort of rough track by the time we found another recess. It was impossible to view it standing up, for it was too shallow, so I sat down and propped my feet against a stone. Below, the precipice dropped down sheer. I looked around. Above, below, and quite near us were pictures; pictures, as I thought, until then unknown. We were overcome with excitement and joy. It was one of those moments when the searcher feels he is, so to speak, moving over an ice-field that no human foot has ever trodden. I called out for the guide; he was quite close by, but he said that he did not know of this recess or of its pictures.

There are women's figures here and men's—huntsmen's. There is one man: he is armed with bow and arrows and he is taking careful aim at something down in the valley. Behind him is a further supply of arrows. In a flash the meaning and significance of the picture became clear to me. It was just so that, in prehistoric times, the huntsman crouched up here; his spare arrows were behind him . . . and down below was the quarry. This sacred recess has not changed throughout the millennia. The sun has shone upon it, the rain has moistened its surface, yet it has remained intact. The picture displays the same colors, it is, in fact, quite the same as it was thousands of years ago

Archer: Painting in red. One-third actual size. Valltorta Ravine, near Albocácer, Province of Castellón de la Plana, Spain.

when the huntsman took aim up here. Below, down there in the ravine, was the game, some animal or other. The man raises his arms, grabs something from behind him, tautens his body, and an arrow goes whirring through the air.

It is astounding that on occasions like this time can stand still for us. This picture was painted maybe ten thousand years ago, yet it looks so lifelike that you can almost imagine you could shake hands with the huntsman of those far-off days. Perhaps he it was who painted himself, kneeling on one knee, his body bent forward, his foot propped against a stone. Now he stretches stealthily to snatch his bow while his other hand reaches for the arrow . . . a snapshot of the chase, a snapshot maybe a hundred centuries old.

I set to work to make some drawings. The effect of this marvelous picture is due to a whole assemblage of cunningly curved lines, of tiny oscillations, of hardly visible movements. The head especially stands out in a wonderfully distinct way. When I had finished drawing I took a good look around and discovered, first of all, a very small figure—no larger than one's thumb—the figure of a squatting man with a pointed beard. And then, after that, there was another one. . . .

(It was later on in Barcelona that I learned from Professor Bosch-Gimpera, the director of the Museum, that he knew of this recess I had "discovered." It had, furthermore, a name, the Cueva Saltadora, but the paintings in it had not been all copied or photographed and only a small number of them had been published. There and then, Bosch-Gimpera gave me permission to publish those which had not already been given to the public.)

Again this day we set off, uphill and downhill, through scrub and thick bushes. In another recess we saw the picture of a hunter who, pierced with arrows, is falling to the ground. But one leg is shown; the hand is pressed against the knee. He is still grasping his bow with his right hand, but the enemy arrow has already struck its fatal blow. His life is fast ebbing away.

We clambered along from recess to recess and saw more and more paintings. There are altogether fifteen painted sites in Valltorta. Yet neighboring valleys of similar appearance and possessing comparable niches or recesses in the rock-face show not a single prehistoric drawing or painting. The Valltorta Ravine must have been a very special gorge, a gorge of wizards, a gorge where men might be blessed with luck in the chase, a gorge dedicated and sacred to hallowed activities.

At midday it was so hot that it was long before we could find a shady spot in which to eat our luncheon. We did however light upon a patch of shadow behind a boulder, but we had to lie down if we would keep our heads out of the sunlight. We opened up the basket. It contained country bread as hard as a brick, and cold tortillas or omelettes; besides that there was some red wine—and nothing else. We soon drank up all the wine. Then the heat bore down upon us heavier than ever. The sun burned pitilessly. The sky was like brass, cloudless, shimmering. We were so tired that we had to rest a long time, then at last we got off again . . . uphill, downhill, and then uphill again.

During the afternoon we felt our tongues burning and our palates desiccated. We must have something to drink. Our guide pulled the red-wine bottle out of the basket and ran with it up the hill. It was not long before we could spy him milking a cow into the bottle. He came back, beaming. The fresh milk put new life into us all.

As twilight came on we turned to walk back to Albocácer, and although we took a road different from that we had followed in the morning we had a good four hours' tramp before us. We were, indeed, already tired when we started back, for the day had been particularly fatiguing. Our track home lay through the river's dale, the glen, the vale, but there was never any sort of path; our way lay over stones, by boulders, and through scrub. Even the guide was exhausted. After three hours' walking we were almost at the end of our tether. In the darkness we fumbled along. Once we struck the high road the going was a little better, but our feet dragged, as heavy as lead.

When we glimpsed the lights of Albocácer it was midnight. The guide was so jaded that he could hardly pronounce the words "Good night." It was very, very slowly indeed that we climbed up the stairs to our room, for our knees were stiff and our legs rigid. But, still, all the time the picture, the figure of the hunter was before my eyes, the hunter who was looking down into the ravine and shooting—millennia ago. The words of the old hymn came into my mind: "A Thousand Ages in Thy Sight . . ."

X: Niaux

Ground plan of the Niaux Cavern, near Tarascon-sur-Ariège, Ariège Department, France: (1) Entrance. (2) Main hall with paintings. (3) Engravings on the ground. (4) Engravings. (5) Engravings. (6) Subterranean Pool.

The lecture room is in darkness. Suddenly, a slide is projected on the screen and, there, on the white surface, is a wild horse from the Niaux cavern near Tarascon-sur-Ariège up in the foothills of the Pyrenees. One can sense that the whole audience is enthralled. At least I know that I am fascinated by this age-old art. See how the muzzle is pushed forward, how marvelously the eye is rendered, how the ear stands pricked up and, most remarkable of all, how the mane of the beast is dashed off with a few light strokes and how the long hairs under the jaw are represented so that they stand out as though one could touch them. The whole painting shows astounding facility and sureness of drawing at the service of a clearly conceived intention.

The scene was the University of Mainz and the year was 1949. The lecture room was crammed with eager, tense faces leaning forward in the direction of the screen. In a flash, the thought came to me. What if this audience could be shown the original? What if one could transport this roomful of students off to Niaux, to see the original of this picture? These budding prehistorians would in that way learn and realize far more than by just looking at a slide thrown upon a screen. I reflected that in the thirties I had often taken parties of my students from Cologne University to Niaux. Surely the same sort of pilgrimage must be possible today? And, thereupon, thinking out loud, I said, "You must come with me and stand before the original, you must come to France, to Paris, to Toulouse, and then up to Niaux in the mountains."

On hearing my fanciful speech the audience burst out laughing, for my caprice, as it sounded to them, appeared quite impossible to carry out. It was certainly four years after the end of the war, but Germans could obtain neither passports nor foreign exchange. No one could travel abroad, and here I was babbling about taking students to visit caves in France! Obviously, the whole thing was too good to be true. Still, once I had got the idea into my head I could not get rid of it so I went, first of all, to see Monsieur Fosse, the liaison officer between the University and the French official administration, and put the question up to him. Was such a plan possible, or impossible, to carry out? He seemed pleased with my idea and promised to do all he could to help.

With so much encouragement we were able to go ahead and make up a preliminary program. Then the good news came rolling in. General Schmittlein supported the project. The French Foreign Minister gave his special approval.

The German and French state railways allowed us considerable reductions in fares while the municipal authorities of the city of Toulouse got a motor-bus for us. We were to meet it at Brive, about halfway to Toulouse on the railway line from Paris. All was set for an eight days' tour through France. On all sides we got price reductions, favors, and privileges of different sorts. The Toulouse *Syndicat d'Initiative* looked after getting us hotel rooms, meals, guides for the caves, and everything we needed—right down to lamps. Every day that went by saw our project take firmer shape and form. The necessary foreign exchange was obtained. We wrote any number of letters to French prehistorians and to local archaeologists, to government offices and to the French railway authorities, to the Toulouse municipal council and to the university of that city as well as to the University of Paris. Little by little all the very real and numerous difficulties were ironed out.

The meeting-place for twenty students and myself was Mainz railway station and the date was October 4, 1949. With us also were Drs. Klumbach and Menzel from the Romano-German Museum in Mainz. And, except for myself, none of the party had ever visited France before. War, and the immediate postwar difficulties, had put foreign travel out of the question for over a decade. So, indeed, all of us felt that we were dreaming we were moving about inside a fairy story. We were going to France and all through France right down to the Pyrenees—on the Spanish frontier. All around me were beaming faces, and it was a pleasing thought that some, at least, of the students who were at the lecture were going to see the original of the picture, were going to Niaux.

It was almost dark when our train pulled out of Mainz station, and it was night when we crossed the frontier. At dawn we were in Paris, where we stayed three days. We paid some visits to scientists who, in the most friendly fashion, showed us through their museums. We saw the Museum of National Antiquities at Saint-Germain, the Louvre,

Notre-Dame, the Sainte-Chapelle, we went up the Eiffel Tower and walked up the hill to the Sacré-Coeur—and at the sidewalk cafés we refreshed ourselves from the fatigues of sightseeing!

Then, off to Toulouse. The motor-bus was waiting for us at Brive all right. Madame Gibert, representing the Toulouse *Syndicat d'Initiative*, was there to meet us and we had a very nice chauffeur. We set off for Montignac and the Lascaux cave, to which a good motor-road now allows cars to drive right up. Indeed, the visitors' automobiles formed a ceaseless stream. Three days we stayed at Les Eyzies, seeing Font-de-Gaume and Les Combarelles.

Then our way led through Souillac, Cahors, and Moissac with its marvelous cloister and Romanesque church rich in sculpture. Then Carcassonne, the huge, wonderfully well-preserved, though of course largely restored, medieval city-fortress. After that our route lay through Toulouse to Tarascon-sur-Ariège in the Pyrenees.

The countryside got more and more hilly; moderately high hills at first and then, suddenly, the gigantic, towering chain of the Pyrenees. Bumping along over a very twisty road with many steep gradients we at last reached Tarascon. There M. Robert, the president of the Ariège Prehistoric Society, was awaiting us. He had already got the guide for us; his name was Clastres and he knew me quite well, for he had already shown me through Niaux no less than three times. But I felt that this occasion was a much more important one than the others. Here I was with some of my students, and I was going to be able to show them the originals of the far-famed Niaux paintings. We were to stand before these marvels and discuss the problems they suggested. It was a great day for me.

M. Clastres got up into the motor-bus with us, and we then drove along up the high road to a point where the path leads off up to the cavern's mouth. It is almost half an hour's tough climb up to the entrance, and as the path is quite narrow we had to follow one another in Indian file.

All about us rose the high mountains. Right opposite us, there on the other side of the Vicdessos torrent's deep vale, was a mark on the hillside, the opening leading into the La Vache cavern. In it Robert has excavated and has found some really remarkable works of art: engraved bones of very fine workmanship, bison, aurochs, wild horses, even trees—and these are very rare in palaeolithic art. Behind a fold in the valley's walls lies another grotto called Bédeilhac which contains polychrome paintings and some reliefs, all of Ice Age date. But the most beautiful of the painted pre-historic caverns in the French Pyrenean region is undoubt-edly Niaux—and that was where we were headed.

No one spoke. On either side of our path straggled some scrub and low bushes. The precipitous mountain itself is almost bare and, as we made our way along, our feet often loosened little stones that went tumbling and rolling down into the valley far below.

At last we saw an opening but it was so small, and so hard to identify, that without a guide we should never have found it. While the acetylene lamps were being lighted we sat and rested for a few minutes on stones and boulders before the cavern's mouth. Then we heard Clastres's voice, "Everything in order, we can get going now. . . ."

The sun was sinking toward the hill-crests, but it does not matter at what hour you visit Niaux. In it, day is night and night is day, a year, a century or a millennium, all one. As you enter time seems to stand still and a mantle of eter-nity wraps itself around you. Indeed, in my opinion, quite one of the most impressive effects you feel inside the great caverns is that "time" is a concept really devoid of sense and meaning, that everything which we have around us is illusion, that all which usually moves and sways us has lost importance and value.

First of all the ground leads steeply upward as one's eyes, very gradually, get accustomed to the darkness. We had only four lamps among more than twenty people, for it is not very often that so large a party visits the cave. Niaux, indeed, is not nearly so well arranged for visitors as is Lascaux. The former is isolated among high hills and only a comparatively few people come to see this group of Pyrenean grottoes, of which, as I have said, Niaux is undoubtedly the finest.

Soon the configuration of the cavern grows imposing and strange. Not far from the entrance is a narrow passage leading out of the large hall. You can see that in former times there was a subterranean lake here, for the line of the banks is marked by stones and pebbles. The ground is damp and slippery. Great care must be exercised or you go slithering down on your back. Now and then drops fall from the walls. A plop of water strikes an uncanny note in the intense silence.

None of us felt inclined to talk so we plodded along without saying a word, one after another. The lamps cast but a meager light and we had to keep well up with each other so as not to lose contact.

The walls of the caves are composed of a variety of rocks. Sometimes they are yellowish and porous as sandstone, then again, without any transition, they will look like marble, the color of old gold—hard, shiny, impervious. Many of the chambers are fairy-tale palaces, stalactites hanging down to the stalagmites that rise to meet them. In places there is water enclosed by banks formed in the course of millennia. One cannot recognize a pool, a pond, or a puddle in the gloom, and we had to pass the word along when our guide had called out a warning. We went on and on. After about half an hour Clastres stopped and swung his light toward the walls covered, at that spot, with red dots and P-shaped signs. Maybe the P-signs depict boomerangs and have, perhaps, the same signification as the arrows which menace so many of the beasts' figures and forms. On again. Clastres stops once more. Now we can clearly see a corral toward which a beast is being driven. Forward. The walls flash up in the jerky light of lamp-

flares. Here the roof is a vast vault soaring up high above
our heads—a hundred feet, a hundred and fifty feet, and
more . . . while the hall itself is of gigantic size. After
that, we must scramble and clamber over a great sand-
dune piled up by the subterranean waters of past ages. On
the height our guide calls a halt. The light-beams illuminate
part of the walls and we can make out how a natural bulge
or boss on the rock was wrought and fashioned into the
likeness of some beast. A protuberance is the animal's back
while the rest of the body has been painted in. The creature stands out from the walls in an extraordinary combination of natural relief and man's handiwork.

The party moved on. Clastres halted once more. He
pointed to the wall where there were red-paint marks, two
arrows, one pointing downward and the other upward.
Clastres said, "No one knows what these arrows mean
nor why one is directed up and the other down."

The trail of men in darkness within a mountain. The trail
led on and with each step the atmosphere grew more uncanny. Intense stillness. Nothing but the dull thud of footsteps, which echoed against the walls of the caverns. Ghostlike, the lights danced and flickered. At last we arrived at
the farthermost of the great halls.

It is roughly circular, like some gigantic round shrine
under a cupola. Here it is that the largest and finest paintings are preserved. We are upon them before we know it.
All at once we are staring at great pictures, from three to
six feet long, painted in black against the light, fawn-
colored walls of the chamber.

A bison, then another. An ibex . . . a large wild horse
. . . and, look there, the painting that was the excuse and
the motive for all our pilgrimage, the wild horse with the
impressive forequarters and head.

We stood quite silent before this marvelous assemblage,
this splendid collection of prehistoric masterpieces. We
were all too anxious to behold what we had come to see

for any of us to be inclined to comment. And what we had come to see were examples of a perfect and most ancient art.

There is no trace of restriction, but everything is developed from the inner content of the figure, from within the object. Quite thin strips of stalagmitic matter have, in some places, trickled across the paintings and lie as streaks of glittering crystals over them. Were it not for these witnesses of great antiquity, one might feel inclined to think some modern artist had executed the Niaux pictures. And we are puzzled to imagine how such an art as this could have existed.

"I think we're all extraordinarily lucky to have been able to see these marvels," remarked Dr. Menzel, who was standing just behind me. "I had no idea at all the things were anything like this, and I've studied all the photographs. I'd no idea the reality was so overwhelming."

And again we turned our lamps' light toward the paintings, and again with every fresh glance we could notice new features. The whole of the Niaux assemblage is mid-Magdalenian, admittedly the peak-period of Ice Age art, the pictorial period set between the preceding, linear Aurignacian and the succeeding late Magdalenian art, which is linear again. Still, at Niaux no colors were used. Everything is executed in black pigment; in fact, the paintings give the impression of drawings, though the color was applied with a brush.

We moved on and examined still more pictures in the same chamber and of the same period. Figures of bisons with more large-sized arrows. There is a bison standing. It is boldly, even dashingly, executed, the bushy fur on the beast's back and the hair beneath the muzzle . . . the head is lowered as though in attack. The horns, drawn in perspective, are directed forward. It is quite uncanny how the animal stares at the onlooker, how its glance follows him as he walks away . . . there is a big, heavily built wild horse drawn with free but carefully calculated strokes. The crea-

Bison, red dots, and boomerangs. One-tenth actual size. Niaux Cavern, near Tarascon-sur-Ariège, Ariège Department, France.

ture's muzzle is hairy, the legs clumsy, the mane stands up and does not lie down as it does with tame horses. Every detail has been carefully and acutely observed and then reproducd in masterly fashion. Again and again you feel that you must be dreaming, that you are the victim of some hallucination, that such things just cannot be. So accomplished an art cannot be so ancient and could not be executed with such skill and refinement. Before each new picture cries of admiration escaped the students. It was easy to see that the impression made upon them by the whole assemblage was immense.

Right over there, now, in the wall is a shallow depression; it is about as high up as the level of a man's eyes . . . an opening in the rock-face. Curiously enough, that concavity assumes the form of a stag's head, and then we look hard at the thing and perceive, painted on either side, antlers. So here a real stag's head had been, so to speak, latent, inherent in the concavity; and the painted addition to, or completion of, the image most probably indicates that this spot was especially sacred and holy. Otherwise, why should Old Stone Age Man have perfected a stag's head upon the walls? We may think, of course, of several reasons, but we may be sure that a determining one was something connected with sacrifice, rite, and sacred ritual.

As a matter of fact, this great cave is really a great shrine hallowed in remote antiquity. A gigantic cupola rises to a height of from a hundred and fifty to two hundred feet above the frieze of paintings. The sanctuary is therefore much more lofty than any chamber made with hands. Like Lascaux and Altamira and many other subterranean caverns and grottoes, Niaux was a religious center for Ice Age Man.

Very few questions were put to me; though, from time to time, a few soft, muffled words lost themselves in the cavern's immensity. A cave in a mountain. True enough, but also a numinous place, one still invested with a sacred aura.

Not one of us was willing to depart, but Clastres urged us to turn back whence we had come. We took one last walk round, we stared up again, we gazed our farewell to the pictures, and lingered some time before the horse whose picture brought us hither.

Then we began the journey back.

Once again the silent file of men swung their lamps through the crystal chambers. Light caught in the bizarre conformation of the walls, in the concavities and on the bosses of the vaults. Shadows scurried over the ground while silence hung heavy upon us, like a burden. We were still steeped in gloom, in mystery; we were still under the impression of eternity reflected in these great halls and galleries.

I kept on thinking of the lake that lies at the far end of Niaux, a good deal farther in than the round sanctuary with the paintings. Years before I had visited these still waters. They are more than thirteen hundred yards from the entrance, while the paintings are not more than nine hundred yards in.

This lake is one of the most sinister things to be found

in any of the subterranean grottoes, and when M. Clastres
and I had reached it we sat down on a stone by its edge.
Black and deathly quiet the waters stretched before us.
The absolute stillness by the lakeside is so uncanny that it
soon becomes almost unbearable. One is surrounded by pre-
monitions of dread. Life is timeless and, what is more
alarming, motionless. So profound is the quiet that one can
feel one's very heartbeat. This sitting by the strand of a
subterranean lake is a unique experience. There is always
movement around us. Something or other is always happening. Even in the depth of night there is noise. Leaves shiver,
some beast will stir. You hear a house floor creak, you see
the twinkling of a star, the wind comes blowing or a field
mouse rustles through the grass. But by the banks of the
pool in Niaux nothing stirs. If I had been alone on that
occasion I believe that I should have broken down. Anxiety
would have gripped me too tightly. A stillness, an immo-
bility, a timelessness man cannot endure. And I could recollect the relief we felt when a drop of water plopped down
from the vault above onto the surface of the lake. Something had happened. A sense of salvation. Faint, circular
ripples ringed outwards toward the banks. Then again, all
was still. So had the underground waters lain throughout
the millennia: black, immobile, uncanny, awful.

I reminded M. Clastres of our adventure, and he told
me that he had never been able to rid himself of that day's
memories.

Quietly we moved along our trail. Occasionally one or
another of us slipped or stumbled against a stone, but no
one spoke. We were all enthralled by our impressions.
When we got to the entrance and out into the open air, it
was as though we had been restored to life. Perhaps men of
the Old Stone Age felt things in much the same way when
they emerged from the sacred grottoes. Of course, it was
feelings such as these which hallowed the caverns in whose
painted recesses men did not live. There is no habitation-
floor or stratum at Niaux at all.

The night is dark and blazes with stars. The thin sickle of the moon is high above the hills on the far side of the Vicdessos Valley, high above the hills that rise up and away into lofty mountains. From down below comes up to us the creaking of a farm cart and the brawling swirl of the torrent. We breathe freely again. We are refreshed by the wind. And the stars; they are a salving grace.

XI: Bédeilhac

*Ground plan of the Bédeilhac Cave, near Tarascon-sur-Ariège,
Ariège Department, France: (1) Entrance. (2) Paintings. (3)
Red signs. (4) Engraving on the ground. (5) and (6) Paintings.*

When I opened the shutters the next morning the
autumn sun came streaming into my bedroom at
Tarascon-sur-Ariège. A veil of thin mist draped the mountains, delicate dewdrops glistened on the leaves. I took a
deep breath of the pure morning air, the fresh mountain
air of the Pyrenees. Below me the little river rushed noisily
on its way. It was good to be alive and, then, this was
going to be an eventful day.

Up there, in those mountains that seemed so near, men

of the Ice Age had lived. There they had their caverns and there prehistoric man had waged a hard struggle for subsistence and existence. For all his needs he depended upon animals, so he must, without respite, hunt and track, lay traps and snares, prepare corrals. It was man's cunning, as well as his courage, that enabled him to kill a quarry so often much bigger and stronger than himself. Mammoths, for instance, could, quite obviously, not be mastered by means of bows and arrows, lances, or harpoons. For such bulky beasts deep pits must be dug and covered with branches and small stones. And, then, the creatures' suspicions must not be aroused, but the mammoths driven with such care and art that they tumbled into the pitfall. The stakes were high. If the chase was fruitless, then the tribe went hungry. Everything, then, must be done to insure luck in the hunt. It was the task of the shaman, wizard, or magician to bring luck. He must paint animal figures upon a cave wall, and he must paint them very true to life, else they would be of little or no avail when enchantments were pronounced over them, and arrows or other missiles shot against the pictures.

Down in the dining-room the students were already sitting at their breakfasts. When we had said good morning, there broke out a chorus of inquiries about Bédeilhac, the prehistoric cave we were to visit that day. I sat down and then tried to answer.

"You know this cave's been recognized as a prehistoric site for quite a long time. As far back as 1910 Cartailhac wrote an account of it in the journal L'Anthropologie. In those days, however, only a few red-ochre dots and lines had been recognized. It was not until between 1925 and 1927 that the first polychrome pictures were described.

"And there has been a good deal of digging. Some time about 1930 a M. Mandemant conducted an excavation which laid bare a very well preserved Magdalenian stratum that yielded a considerable number of small art-objects, among which was a human figure with a cowl or hood and pierced through with a hole. The thing must have been used as a pendant. Then there was also a horse's head in stone and a small staff with the representation of another horse's head. The human figure, that of a woman, and a clothed woman too, aroused much interest, since sculptures of the human form are rare among palaeolithic works of art. Taken all together, not more than a hundred and twenty-six of them are known. The finds made at Bédeilhac are now in the Chicago Museum."

When we got out into the street, M. Robert was waiting for us. He it was who conducted the excavations at the La Vache cave, on the other side of the valley and opposite Niaux. There he was very lucky indeed, and came across some splendid things: small pieces of bone with delightful engravings—among them is a bison's head surrounded with pine branches. This is a peculiar assemblage, otherwise un-known in Ice Age art. Maybe the branches indicate a snare for game, an enclosure into which the hunted quarry was driven.

We went up to Monsieur Robert's flat where he told us something about his digging.

"Excavation had been going on, sporadically, for about fifty years, and the site appeared to be exhausted, but I discovered that under the lowest of the excavated layers was not, as had been thought and stated, bed-rock, but a stratum of stalagmitic matter which, in the course of thou-sands of years, had taken on a granite-like hardness. For a long time I debated whether I ought or ought not to dig under this calcite layer until, one day, I just broke it up and disclosed underneath a mid-Magdalenian filling."

"What makes you so sure of the identification? Did you find artifacts?"

Robert went to one of his cases and took out harpoons and stone implements in typical mid-Magdalenian style.

"Yes, all right; now I'm quite convinced these things are certainly mid-Magdalenian."

"And," went on Robert, "close beside those things lay

this piece of bone engraved with a drawing," and with these words he opened a box and disclosed something precious, for it was wrapped in cotton-wool.

"Did you find anything else?" I asked as I bent over the object and admired the delicate beauty of the engraving. For an answer he produced two other short sticks of bone, both engraved in fine, mid-Magdalenian style. It is always a joy to be able to examine such things, evidence of most ancient art, and evidence, moreover, that is dated unimpeachably by the stratum which served as a hiding-place. For such pieces are not only dated themselves but serve to date the wall-paintings which are of similar technique, tradition, and style.

M. Robert's treasures were passed round for the students to examine. Each piece went from hand to hand as though it were a precious jewel. We talked for some time about Magdalenian art, about the huge output of the ancient artists, about the existence of art-schools where students were taught and practiced their arts, and about artists' sketches which served as models for the great wall-pictures.

"While you were digging you never saw engravings or paintings at La Vache?"

"No, never," replied Robert. "I've spent weeks and weeks in the cave. I've examined all the walls very closely, but I've never found anything. If you remember, you yourself went there with me once and you couldn't see anything. No, La Vache must have been a dwelling-place. The sanctuaries, shrines, and holy recesses were adorned with pictures and there men never dwelt. The painted caverns were where the sacred mysteries were transacted and where hallowed rites were performed before the chase."

Our bus was already waiting for us on the main square of the town and our goal was the Bédeilhac grotto where Robert has also excavated and where he discovered a neolithic skeleton. The bus rumbled away over the bridge and then headed up into the mountains. The highway was very twisting and twining and pulled steeply uphill. Soon we were able to make out a gaping entrance.

We had M. Rauzy with us. He is one of the most active of the local excavators. His knowledge of Bédeilhac is un-rivaled and he had very kindly promised to lead us into the farthest and most remote corners of the cavern.

When we got to the entrance we were rather surprised to find that the big motor-bus and its complement of twenty passengers pushed right on and did not stop until it was a good way into the cave, for this cavern has none of the usual little apertures leading into its marvels but, rather, a gigantic opening worthy of a cathedral. Bédeilhac is no less than eight hundred yards long; moreover, during the last few years, side-passages have been discovered lead-ing off from the right of the cavern proper, and in these new galleries also pictures have been found.

The ground is slippery and there are many puddles scat-tered about over the floor, while water drops from the vault. The light from the entrance soon fails and, further-more, there is no prepared path through the cave since it is seldom visited, for neither paintings nor engravings are numerous. Several of us carried acetylene lamps, but they yielded only a faint light, and we had to be very careful to stay well within touch of one another, so as not to get lost. At one point there was a fascinating view. Con-tinual dropping of water from the vault has, in the course of ages, produced something like a fountain, a quite large fountain, in fact. There is a wide base of pyramidal shape set in the middle of a basin which retains the water that has percolated through the roof. Hanging down from the vault is a pendentive of stalactite which is suspended above the pyramidal base. The whole thing is a marvelous freak of nature. It is hard to believe that it is not man's handi-work.

Farther on, the cave becomes quite fairy-like. The walls are dead white, all their jagged points and prongs and spikes eerie in the twilight. We moved on silently until we reached a spot where we had to crouch down under an overhanging curtain of rock. Drawn upon the floor of the grotto here is an astonishingly well preserved head of a horse. It is quite small but displays evidence of great skill in execution. You would say this head is a living thing. The beast seems to be roaring out, neighing aloud when struck by the fatal arrow. And there is only the head, nothing more—it is fascinating to observe how just one light stroke in the clay of a cavern-floor creates an animal's eye, and when one reflects that this thing is not on a wall—and therefore more or less protected—but right in the ground, one can only rejoice that this picture has been preserved through the millennia. And, not far away from the horse's head, there is the figure of a bison also executed in the clay of the floor.

The existing pictures at Bédeilhac are small engravings but they are most impressive. There were, however, once upon a time, large paintings upon the walls of the inner-most recesses, but these pictures have almost entirely disappeared, though here and there traces of pigment indicate that Magdalenian man at Bédeilhac not only engraved but painted as well.

We traced our way back in silence, our feet constantly slipping in the puddles. We skidded about, we held each other's hands, we bent down and crept through narrow passages and then straightened up again to wander through the huge, fantastic halls of a dream-palace. With every visit to prehistoric caverns the visitor experiences an adventure that grips his very soul.

Off in our bus again and to drive through the incomparable scenery of the Pyrenees; little villages, isolated homesteads, majestic trees, far-reaching views over heights, foothills, and peaks. Hardly any fields. The countryside is too harsh for much cultivation or crops, but it holds a bewitching quality. It must be the light. Southern daylight is deeper, stronger, clearer, louder than ours in the north.

The color, the softness, the glitter of this southern light penetrates everything. The shadows here are very sharp, the contrasts most marked. Everything around us has more depth, more luminosity, a more lively life . . . and the joyousness aroused by this light spread among us and filled our hearts.

A most extraordinary thing. The light here is not unrestrained, it does not riot in a tropical glare and yet it has none of the weakness that makes our northern gloom mysterious. This southern light is clear. It neither beautifies nor does it flatter. It reveals. There is a tree and there an isolated farm. A shepherd driving his sheep before him. A town. Each with its own individual existence in this most luminous light: the house, the roof, the mount, the man. And in this individuality lies a mystery which we all feel. In fact, it informs our whole being.

We gaze at the landscape. The motor-bus rolls along.

I sat next to M. Rauzy. Suddenly he asked me: "Do you think that any clear stages of evolution can be recognized in prehistoric art? It always strikes me as so puzzling, uncanny even."

"It's true enough that it's often uncanny in the caverns, but prehistoric art is not, of itself, eerie or sinister; as a matter of fact, I find that it's close to nature, to reality."

"But what were the phases of Ice Age art?"

"Well, it seems to have begun in Aurignacian times. The characteristic style of the epoch is linear—just outlines. No attempt to tackle the problems of perspective, mass, movement."

"The mid-Magdalenian was the high-water mark of prehistoric art?"

"Yes, the apogee of late palaeolithic art occurred in mid-Magdalenian times, and specifically in Magdalenian III and IV. It's to those ages that we must attribute the great paintings of Altamira, Font-de-Gaume, La Pasiega, and some of the Lascaux pictures."

"Do you think, then, that the larger paintings, for instance, at Lascaux, are of later date than Magdalenian III or IV?"

"Yes, I'd say so; they seem to me to reflect the style of the later Magdalenian phases, when linear forms again appeared—forms rather like, even very like, the Aurignacian, but slicker, looking more like the work of virtuosi, more dextrous; the essential is conveyed with a few bold and decisive strokes."

"We've got the same sort of thing in modern art."

"Of course, and that seems to me perhaps the most marvelous thing about the whole story—modern Impressionism very much resembling Ice Age art. They are both art-traditions, modes, if you will, with discontinuous contour-lines, with similar bold, light brush-strokes. Artists of both phases, both epochs divided from one another by millennia, were preoccupied with the same problems relating to space, depth, perspective, movement, mass, and the instantaneous view. As an example of what I mean, there is a small length of bone (from Teyjat) engraved with the representation of a herd of deer in movement, advancing. Not each individual deer is drawn, but—just as with the Impressionists—the whole group, the mass of beasts is conveyed by means of a number of similar strokes suggesting antlers. Only the first animal on the left and the last three on the right are clearly and fully delineated. It's just the Impressionist technique—and there's another engraving much the same as the Teyjat piece; it's from Chaffaud."

Here one of the students joined in the conversation: "After Impressionism, Expressionism . . . is there any Expressionism in prehistoric art?"

"Yes, I should say certainly. As Expressionism strives more and more after 'expression,' as simplification is more and more sought after, pictorial art becomes more and more flat. No attempt is made to convey the effect of depth in space . . . well, you've got all those things in the Levantine Spanish art. In the Valltorta Ravine, at

Minateda, Alpera, and Cogul, the pictures lie exposed on rock-faces above ground and are not hidden, as are the palaeolithic masterpieces, in deep, subterranean caverns . . . the Levantine pictures, as you know, display elongated human figures, men running, hurrying, jumping, leaping, men in vigorous movement."

"I can follow that, but if there's Expressionism there's surely no Cubism?"

Advancing herd of reindeer: Engraving on bone. Actual size. Teyjat, Dordogne Department, France.

"Oh, yes, there is. There's Cubism too. That's one of the things that's so astounding in this parallelism between modern and prehistoric art. Cubism existed millennia ago, and it's so Cubist, so informed with the spirit of abstract art, that prehistoric art appears even more Cubist than our own Cubism."

"But where are these ancient Cubist pictures to be found?"

"Well, in central Spain and in southern Spain, particularly in the Sierra Morena. There we find rock-pictures on surfaces under rock-shelters, pictures exposed to sunlight and wind but, despite that, keeping their colors to this day. In many places it can be clearly recognized that these drawings and designs have their roots in upper palaeolithic art; indeed, that these pictures are Impressionistic versions of Ice Age 'originals.' Over these we find paintings in the style of the Levantine Spanish rock-frescoes, while, over all, come the wholly stylized designs of neolithic and chalcolithic date; that is, between about 2500 and 800 B.C."

"So modern art is developing in the same directions as did prehistoric art?"

"Well, what I'd care to say would be that Impressionism, Expressionism, and Cubism are three phases which appear always to follow, the one behind the other."

"But after Cubism, there's something more," put in another student. "Prehistoric art did not just stop at the Cubist stage; we can, after that phase, see art-evolution in reverse, so to say."

"Yes, you're quite right there," I replied. "Prehistoric Cubism was so abstract that pictures are sometimes reduced to a triangle or to just an angle: in fact, the human figure is broken up or dissolved into Cubist forms, just as in the case of the modern Cubist painters. It is probable that such prehistoric pictures are intended to represent demons, spirits, monsters. They are more sinister than men, because while closely related to human nature, and partaking even of human substance, they have no human form. Thus prehistoric Cubism originated on a transcendental plane, in a realm of the spirit lying beyond our senses, while Impressionism has its roots in this visible world around us, whether it be the Impressionism of late palaeolithic times or that of 1900.

"It looks as though there must also recur the movement in the other direction. After the Cubist forms, which reached their fullest expression in Bronze Age times, art gradually once again got more naturalistic—very slowly, it's true, but nevertheless constantly."

"Professor," said another student, "you refer to periods and times with very great certainty, but is it possible to be so sure about the dating of prehistoric pictures?"

"That is a fair enough question, but, as a matter of fact, we often can date very accurately. Sometimes our dead and gone ancestors represented in their pictures something of their possessions—utensils, tools, and the like. To take an example, the picture of a certain dagger indicates Phase

I of the Bronze Age which, in Spain, would be from about 2000 to 1600 B.C. Such dating is confirmed by the evidence of imported objects from Egypt or Crete. So, you see, we've got quite a lot of means of dating the past. The data from various sources can be combined and thus supply cross-checks."

Just at this moment we saw a car pulled up by the side of the road. Those inside it were making signs and calling out to us. When our bus stopped we recognized the son of my old friend Count Bégouen, the veteran explorer of southern French prehistoric caves. It was Louis Bégouen with his sons. He greeted us all in friendly fashion, for I had known him for years; in fact, he had guided me through many caverns which, without his help, I should never have been able to visit. He told us that his father was in good health and was looking forward to our visit.

When the Bégouens drove off we followed their car along the winding and complicated Pyrenean roads as far as the Château des Espas, Count Bégouen's seat. The old gentleman was then eighty-four years of age and still astonishingly active in mind and body.* Thence we went on to the Château de Pujol where Louis Bégouen lives and where his father awaited us.

The sun sank slowly and dyed the whole great Pyrenean chain blood-red. The peaks stood out dark and clear against the blazing sky. We could see far and wide over crests and dales and mountain summits.

A long avenue of chestnut trees leads up to Pujol, lying quite isolated among the hills and surrounded by fine old trees. We got out and followed Louis Bégouen up to the terrace where the old Count was sitting surrounded by members of his family. The old gentleman slowly rose and we all felt that this was a great occasion. Those of the younger generation, who were preparing themselves for a life of research and devotion to science, had an opportunity

---

* Count Bégouen celebrated his ninetieth birthday in 1953 and was, when this book was published, still in excellent health. (*Translator's note*.)

of meeting one of the most distinguished prehistorians and archaeologists of the older generation, a man who has done much to throw light upon man's history.

I now was able to take a good look at my old friend. He had, of course, aged since we had last met. He leaned upon his stick, but his white beard still framed his wise, clever face, his eyes had lost none of their brilliance or their piercing glance. None of the younger people spoke, but the old Count opened his arms wide, embraced me, and kissed me on both cheeks. I was overjoyed at this welcome from an old friend. He looked at us all keenly and then he delivered a short but impressive address in German.

A new generation was growing up, he said, a new generation whose task it would be to continue the work their elders had done to reveal the earlier phases of man's history.

"Many questions remain to be settled. Many hands are needed to toil at a task which, truth to tell, is endless. . . .

His words moved us deeply. I made a reply in French, saying that two wars had interrupted our researches, and even, in some measure, nullified them but, nevertheless, our task was clear enough: to explore what is everlasting and essential in man, and to endeavor to penetrate ever more deeply into the things of the spirit.

XII: Pindal

Ground plan of the Pindal Cavern near Pimiango, Province of Oviedo, Spain: (1) Elephant in red pigment. (2) to (4) Engravings and paintings.

The rain drove steadily against the train's windows. Rain, nothing but rain, and we had imagined that we were on our way to sunny Spain. But there was nothing to remind us of the south and the scenery was more like that of central Germany than we had expected. The climate, too, seemed much the same as that of central Germany—cold, rainy, inhospitable. This eternal rain was getting us down. Our fellow passengers in the compartment vouchsafed the information that, in this part of the world, it rained the whole year round. From their rather weary voices we judged that the rain had made them depressed too.

One of our fellow travelers pointed to a meadow where some vague human forms were moving about. They were wearing strange footgear—in fact they had on stilts, little stilts it is true, but stilts all the same. When the train pulled up at the next little station we could see that here, too, everyone was supplied with stilts, if one can call them that—they are clogs with cleats or struts nearly a foot high. These queer contraptions lend a strange appearance to the whole population, but evidently they are very useful, for everyone was wearing them—men, women, and children.

The rain never ceased for one instant. The pedestrians we could catch sight of walking about the streets were wrapped up in capacious cloaks and, of course, wore the peculiar clogs of the country, a most odd sort of country it seemed to us.

When we had left Santander that morning it had been clear, but as soon as we got up into the mountains the rain started and if it was not a torrential downpour the whole time it never tailed off into what one might call a drizzle. Not a single patch of blue could be seen in the leaden-gray sky. Wet made its way through the sides of the train and everything one touched was damp. All the region near the southern shores of the Bay of Biscay is, indeed, one of the wettest and most rainy spots in the whole of Europe.

We began to get anxious about our excursion to the cave. Even though we had raincoats, still the prospect of more than an hour's walk through a rainstorm was not at all pleasant. Then it struck me that it might be a good idea for us to wear the local clogs. It is always a sound scheme to use the same clothes as the people of the country. They have had plenty of time, hundreds of years, in which to try out various sorts of garments.

The train pulled up at Unquera and we got out. Here, again, everyone wore the Cantabrian clogs; they make their wearers lift their knees up in a stiff and clumsy step. When several of the clog-wearers are together they look like comedians putting on an act. We had some difficulty in not laughing out loud when we saw men, women, and children strutting about in a meadow like marionettes. Marionettes—or perhaps rather some of those wading-birds such as the storks and ibises one sees in Egypt.

We asked about the chances of getting a car for Colombres and on to Pimiango, a hamlet near Pindal Cave. But no one was willing to drive us. I say a car, but the most one could have hoped for was a cart. And we were told that, as there was no real road, the cart would soon get stuck. So, obviously, the thing to do was to buy two pairs of the stilted clogs. Rita and I tried walking our first few steps while we were still in the shop. Everything seemed to be all right, so we decided to do our best to walk up to the cave. With these clogs there is no question of getting along quickly. We had to laugh at our clumsy attempts and awkward movements. It is not nearly such easy going as it looks, for if one sinks in the mud it is quite a job to pull the clogs out of the mire and get going again. In fact, it is a very tiring mode of progression indeed.

Of course it rained all the time. Our hats, coats, and shoes were soon sopping wet, and the unusual mode of walking was so tiring that we had to stop every few paces. Still, the whole thing was so absurd that it kept us in good humor. As we neared Colombres the track got a little better. However, we did not dare to pull off our clogs and there we were stumping along the road, two very queer-looking customers, drenched to the skin.

From Colombres it is a steep pull up to Pimiango, and the going is worse than ever. We often missed the track altogether and when we got to Pimiango we were very sorry for ourselves.

There is only one shop at Pimiango. It stocks everything the local inhabitants need: foodstuffs of all kinds, agricultural implements, and supplies for schoolchildren. The shop is also the local inn and restaurant. The whole place reminded us of Norway. So cold in summer. The peculiar aroma compounded of stockfish, cheese, and brandy. Just like those out-of-the-way hamlets in northern Scandinavia that one comes across when searching for prehistoric rock-pictures.

Besides ourselves there was one other guest at the inn, a Spaniard. In such places one soon gets into conversation with strangers. When the Spaniard learned that we wanted to visit Pindal, he displayed considerable interest and offered to come with us. Both Rita and I were delighted at his proposal, for it looked as though it was going to be unusually difficult to get a guide, and without someone to act as a guide it is often impossible to find the entrances to the caves. The stranger told us his name and added that he was the vicar of Colombres. He would be very pleased to visit the caves in company with his country's guests. The vicar was also wearing the local clogs.

But we were not ready to start at once. We needed some time to get warmed up, dried out, and to recover from the fatigue of our long walk. We had a typically rustic Spanish meal: local Asturian dishes. When we were ready for the climb the vicar got up to accompany us. He was a man in the prime of life. For a Spaniard, rather tall, slender, and with dark eyes and black hair. His conversation was lively and entertaining and he punctuated his speech with plenty of gestures, both of hand and arm. I at once took a liking to him and we soon found common ground for discussion —cave-exploration, men of the Ice Age, the technique of painting, the style of the cave pictures.

"Let's visit the cave," I finally proposed; "we'll let the magic of far-off ages work upon us." And he agreed. Our coats had been fairly well dried out at the inn but our hats were as wet as ever and we had to get up to that cave. As we stepped out of the inn, the first thing we saw was the lighthouse known as Tina Mayor. It rises up, a most imposing massive tower, dominating the countryside. Then

we had not been more than a few minutes on our way
before we heard a strange roaring noise. I asked the priest
what it was. He said it was the thunder of the sea-waves
and that we were quite near to a tall precipice whose sheer
cliffs drop right down into the Bay of Biscay's waters. The
bellow of the waves got even louder. The ground was all
rock and stones. Only here and there, in scanty patches,
was there a little sparse scrub . . . then, quite suddenly,
before us lay the sea—gray, boundless, sinister. The coast
was most abrupt, the rocks indented, and everywhere you
could see inlets, ravines, headlands, declivities, and then
the drop right down to the ocean.

To the ocean beneath us—where the waters rolled and
foamed in a frenzied bellowing and howling. Rains and
storms whipped the sea and piled up the waves house-high
before they hurled themselves against the wall-like cliffs. It
was terrifying to gaze down into the chasm. Everything so
tremendously powerful. Forces much more mighty than
man and the cliffs far beyond his measure. Here, at this
meteorological outpost of Europe, all nature seems more
powerful and more wild than elsewhere in the continent.

Here the southern warm winds and the northern cold
winds meet. How glad we had been, on other occasions,
when traveling by sea, to leave the Bay of Biscay behind
us. Now we were on land and gazing over the gray immensity of the ocean, but its dangers, its might, and its fury
we felt as vividly as though we were at sea.

The roaring was so loud that it was hard to make oneself heard. The vicar pointed out a spot on the rock-face.
We must climb halfway up the cliff and then make our
way to the cavern's mouth that was high above a deep
cleft ravine.

The entrance to Pindal is, indeed, rather less than ten
feet in height. When we had scrambled up we lighted our
lamps, pulled on our woollen sweaters, and began to make
our way in the grotto. We were soon shut off from all
daylight, though the insistent roar of the sea haunted us for

some time longer. Gradually the din grew fainter and then, quite suddenly, ceased altogether. As in all the caverns, a great stillness lay upon us.

The ground was wet and slippery and here, as in so many other caves, we had to join hands so as not to slip or fall. At Pindal there are no archaeological strata; there is no floor of sand, even. Excavations would be utterly fruitless, for bed-rock is everywhere under one's foot. In many spots a few drops of water trickle down from the roof and feed a scanty drain that flows sluggishly through the middle of the cave, while on all sides the stalactites jut down.

At first the going was rather steeply downward, then all at once a gigantic pillar blocked our way. Beautiful spikes and icicles of calcite dripped from the vault—a magic palace, a fairy-story setting, the tale of the Ice Princess by Hans Christian Andersen. And the stillness, the terrifying stillness, broken only, from time to time, by the splash and plop of falling drops that the walls tossed back in faint echoes.

It is clear that Pindal is hardly ever visited. There are practically no traces of modern footsteps upon the ground. Indeed, you might easily enough get the impression that you were the first to enter this most isolated and inaccessible cavern. But, of course, Breuil has given a detailed description of it in his writings.

We had to go up and then go down, to clamber over stones, hummocks, and boulders. When we had got to about a hundred and fifty yards or so from the entrance, the vicar guided us toward the left-hand side wall. A picture of a horse's head executed with bold and powerful strokes in red pigment. The style is typically late Magdalenian—but the drawing is masterly.

We scrambled on farther and farther. Again and again stalagmites barred our path. When we were well over three hundred yards into the heart of the mountain we discovered delicately executed engravings whose thin outlines depicted horses and reindeer. Quite near by was a mass of red dots and a red line scored with red crosslines. This looks rather like a tree.

Pindal ends about four hundred and fifty yards from the entrance. Some way before the end it gets very narrow, so that we had to crouch, creep, and crawl, but in this last, constricted gallery are no pictures, no paintings, nor indeed anything else to bear witness to man's presence.

By this time we were so tired from all our exertions that, in the last of the large chambers, we sat down on a boulder and gazed long at the fabulous beauty of the sur-roundings—of the building, one is tempted to say, so diffi-cult is it to realize that such architectual quality is natural and not man-made.

I mentioned the large-scale elephant in red pigment that is one of the outstanding features of Pindal. The priest got up and pointed it out to us. The painting is on the right-hand side of the cavern and makes a striking impression both from the realistic nature of the figure and also from the bold and sure technique of the drawing. The beast is a powerful pachyderm, measuring roughly two feet long by as much high. Only two legs are shown and the great trunk hangs down nearly to the ground. On the animal's body is a relatively large heart-shaped spot of pigment which, very possibly, represents the physical heart the hunter sought to strike. At El Castillo there is a similar figure— neither at Pindal nor El Castillo is an eye shown, nor more than two legs. The Pindal elephant is nearly five feet above the floor level, so the painting stands out very well. We stayed admiring the picture for a long time.

The work appears to be of Aurignacian date, but al-though, as I have said, the outline is firmly and surely delineated, here and there are signs of discontinuity, of a slight loosening-up, one might say. These are noticeable, for instance, in the treatment of the beast's back and also of its trunk.

We walked on a few paces before we caught sight of a wonderfully well executed fish with quite long fins and a small head. It appears to be a sort of tunny, or at any rate a relation of the tunny and a fish that is now extinct. Under this is the figure of a bison, unfortunately badly damaged and difficult to recognize in its present state. Near by are some more red dots and a Y-shaped sign. Then you can behold the outline of a hind very skillfully painted in red.

On and on we went, closely examining the walls until we came across a large bison both painted and engraved. The pigment has not survived very well but the engraved lines are in perfect preservation and the whole picture is an interesting example of combined painting and engraving by an Ice Age artist.

After that we crept along still farther until we noticed more red signs. Many of them are like sticks or thickened strokes, but they all have swellings or projections on one side. One is at once reminded of boomerangs, which is very possibly what they were intended to represent. A little farther on we discovered a bison, the lower parts of which are engraved, though the beast's back is indicated by a dashing, thick line, while the eye is enlivened with a blob of red pigment. On the body is represented the missile—probably an arrow—which must slay the animal, while, on the right-hand side, two red boomerang-like signs project toward the bison. From below the figure no less than six of the boomerang-like weapons menace the creature. Quite close to this is a drawing with many points or dots which, perhaps, indicate the "bag" or head of game accounted for. Still lower down is the engraving of a horse.

One of the finest, indeed, of all the Pindal pictures is this engraving of a horse's head. The creature was represented as it was falling and with its head stretched forward and upward. Not so far from this we identified yet another horse, very skillfully and carefully engraved. This, again, bore an arrow-mark as well as three dots under the head. Finally, the last of the Pindal prehistoric paintings consisted of strange-shaped signs in red pigment, marks to which it is difficult to assign any interpretation at all.

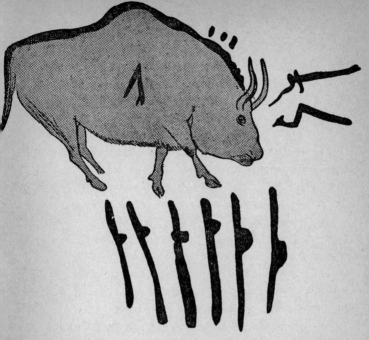

Bison and boomerangs: Painting in Pindal Cave, near Colombres, Province of Oviedo, Spain. One-tenth actual size.

When we got back to the cave's entrance we were thoroughly exhausted from the day's exertions, the long walk and the clambering, creeping, slipping, and scrambling about the cave itself, as well, of course, from the exciting but tiring search for the pictures. The vicar proposed that we should take a long rest just inside the cavern's entrance where the incessant roaring of the sea would not disturb us so much. He asked me how I had liked Pindal and I told him, of course, what was true; namely that we had been fascinated by the great grotto and its picture gallery, for every prehistoric cave offers its own peculiar examples of drawing, style, technique. In order to get material for comparison and appreciation it is necessary to visit as many caves as possible. And I added that for years I had been

ICE AGE CAVE PAINTINGS IN SPAIN

Circles mark the sites of post-Ice Age art finds in eastern Spain

1. Buxu
2. Coberizas
3. La Franca
4. Las Herrerias
5. La Loja
6. Las Mestas
7. Peña de Candamo
8. Pindal
9. Quintanal
10. San Antonio
11. Atapuerca
12. Barcina
13. Los Casares
14. La Hoz
15. La Cala
16. Cueva Dona Trinidad
17. La Pileta
18. Las Aguas
19. Altamira
20. El Castillo
21. Clotilde de Santa
    Isabel
22. Covalanas
23. La Haza
24. Hornos de la Peña
25. La Meaza
26. La Pasiega
27. El Pendo
28. Salitre
29. Santian
30. Sotariza
31. Alquerdi
32. Santimamime
    (Basondo)
33. Venta de la Perra

Eastern Spanish cave paintings later than the Ice Age

1. Alpera
2. Minateda
3. Mugron
4. Cueva de las Grajas
5. Lavaderos de Tello
6. Estrecho de Santonge
7. Cueva Chiquita de
   los Treinta
8. Palomas
9. Pretina
10. Gasulla Gorge
11. Morella la Vella
12. Valltorta Gorge
13. Villar del Humo
14. Tabla de Pochico
15. El Prado del Azogue
16. Cueva del Santo
17. Cogul
18. Cantos de la Visera
19. Benifallet
20. Perelló
21. Tivisa
22. Vandellos
23. Alacón
24. Albarracín
25. Calapatá
26. Chargo del Agua
    Amarga
27. El Secans
28. Tormón
29. Cuevas de la Araña
30. Tortosillas

crouching and clambering through the prehistoric caverns of France and Spain and that I had devoted much of my life to the study of problems connected with the Ice Age.

We sat upon the stone just inside the entrance to Pindal Cave. Without was the crashing thunder of the waves, the blustering howl of the winds. Wrapped round in our cloaks and greatcoats, we stared steadily before us. The roaring of the sea rose ever louder and louder, the wind blew ever more fiercely.

It had become cold. A drizzle was filling the air, night was overtaking us. Through the darkness roared the ocean as it did when men first came this way.

Epilogue

From out of the caverns hidden deep in the recesses of the earth, mysterious things have appeared. Caves have found voices and speak to us about men of long ago, men far off from us and yet so near. Men very like ourselves. Their hopes were comparable to ours, their wishes and their dreams not so very different from our own. What spurred on prehistoric men, what set their tasks, what provided their goal was what we may call the complex of birth and death. The birth of men and beasts—symbolized by the ever recurring representations of pregnant creatures, of copulation. Death—symbolized by the innumerable figures of arrows aimed at or striking the forms of animals, and death, also, invoked by the hallowing and conjuring of pictures and by dances performed before them.

The science of prehistory allows us to glance into the depths. Standing, as it were, on the surface of today, we can look down into the profound pit of our remote past and, there, as in a mirror, see ourselves . . . beings like ourselves. We see man struggling for existence, fighting with the mighty powers to which he is subservient. We realize, all too clearly, that the fond fancy of a Golden Age, of a prehistoric paradise, is but a dream. Man pitted himself against beasts and was untiring in his fight. But from out of this arduous and ardent food-quest arose the great spiritual qualities which have served and still serve us as aid, protection, and encouragement in our own struggle for existence:

First of all, religion, expressed in magic, wizardry, ritual dances, ceremonial garments, enchantment, sacred song . . . and art, close-linked with religion, then as in later epochs. Next, sustained and coherent thought, subjective concepts, magic experience of strange phenomena; a magical conception of the universe. Lastly, we have philosophy. All three realms of the spiritual life—religion, art, and philosophy—have their beginnings in that world of prehistoric man.

Still, before our eyes, as it were, we can see the wondrous evolution of religion, of art, of philosophy, of political organization. And these are the great and fundamental subjects to which this book leads up, the origins of man as Man, something different from all other living creatures.

ICE AGE CAVE PAINTINGS IN FRANCE

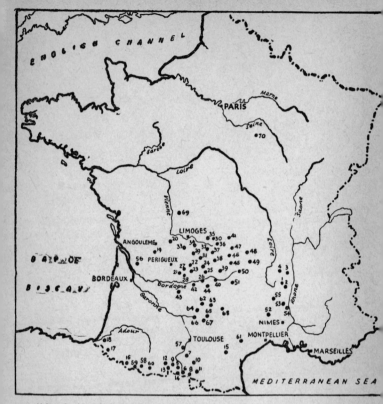

Although the relative position of the various southwestern sites is given, owing to their number they are shown as spreading over much more territory than they do in fact occupy.

1. Baume Pasqualine
2. Le Colombier
3. Ebou
4. Oullins
5. Bédeilhac
6. Lombrive
7. Mas d'Azil
8. Niaux
9. Grotte du Peyort
10. Le Portel
11. Pradières
12. Les Trois-Frères
13. Tuc d'Audoubert
14. Ussat
15. Sallèles-Cabardès
16. Etcheberri
17. Isturitz
18. Jasisiloaga
19. La Chaire à Calvin
20. Le Roc de Sers
21. Barabao
22. Belcayre
23. Bernifal
24. Les Bernous

25. Beyssac
26. La Calévie
27. Cap Blanc
28. Château-La-Tour
29. Comarque
30. Les Combarelles
31. La Croze
32. Delluc
33. La Ferrassie
34. Fongal
35. Font-de-Gaume
36. Fourneau du Diable
37. Le Gabillou
38. Gorge d'Enfer
39. La Grèze
40. Jean-Blancs
41. Lascaux
42. Laugerie Basse
43. Laussel
44. La Mouthe
45. Grotte de Nancy
46. Oreille d'Enfer
47. Roc de la Pépue

48. Sergeac
49. La Sudrie
50. Terme-Pialat
51. Teyjat
52. Bayol
53. Chabot
54. Le Figuier
55. Labaume-Latrone
56. Pair-non-Pair
57. Marsoulas
58. Montespan
59. Gargas
60. Labastide
61. Aldène
62. Cabrerets
63. Cantal
64. Marcenac
65. Grotte des Merveilles
66. Murat
67. Penne d'Albigeois
68. Sainte-Eulalie
69. Angles-sur-Anglin
70. Arcy-sur-Cure

INDEX

(Page numbers in *italic* type refer to illustrations)

Interior by Melanie Kahane, A. I. D.